# YOU TAKE THE HIGH ROAD

# NORTHUMBERLAND WALKS

*With alternative routes
to suit all abilities*

© Anne Leuchars & Debby Waldron, 2014

**All Rights Reserved.** No part of this publication may be reproduced, stored in a retrieval system, or transmitted in any form or by any means – electronic, mechanical, photocopying, recording, or otherwise – without prior written permission from the publisher or a licence permitting restricted copying issued by the Copyright Licensing Agency, 90 Tottenham Court Road, London W1P 0LA. This book may not be lent, resold, hired out or otherwise disposed of by trade in any form of binding or cover other than that in which it is published, without the prior consent of the publisher.

**Moral Rights**: The authors have asserted their moral rights to be identified as the Authors of this Work.

**Published b**y Sigma Leisure – an imprint of
Sigma Press, Stobart House, Pontyclerc, Penybanc Road, Ammanford, Carmarthenshire SA18 3HP.

**British Library Cataloguing in Publication Data**
A CIP record for this book is available from the British Library.

**ISBN**: 978-1-85058-993-8

**Typesetting and Design by**: Sigma Press, Ammanford.

**Cover photograph**: Heading up the Border County Ride © Debby Waldron

**Photographs**: © Debby Waldron

Every effort has been made to fulfil requirements with regard to reproducing copyright material. The authors and publisher will be glad to rectify any ommissions at the earliest opportunity

**Maps**: Sigma Press

**Printed by**: TJ International, Padstow, Cornwall

**Disclaimer**: the information in this book is given in good faith and is believed to be correct at the time of publication. No responsibility is accepted by either the authors or publisher for errors or omissions, or for any loss or injury however caused. Only you can judge your own fitness, competence and experience. Do not rely solely on sketch maps for navigation: we strongly recommend the use of appropriate Ordnance Survey (or equivalent) maps.

# YOU TAKE THE HIGH ROAD
# NORTHUMBERLAND WALKS

## With alternative routes to suit all abilities

### Anne Leuchars & Debby Waldron

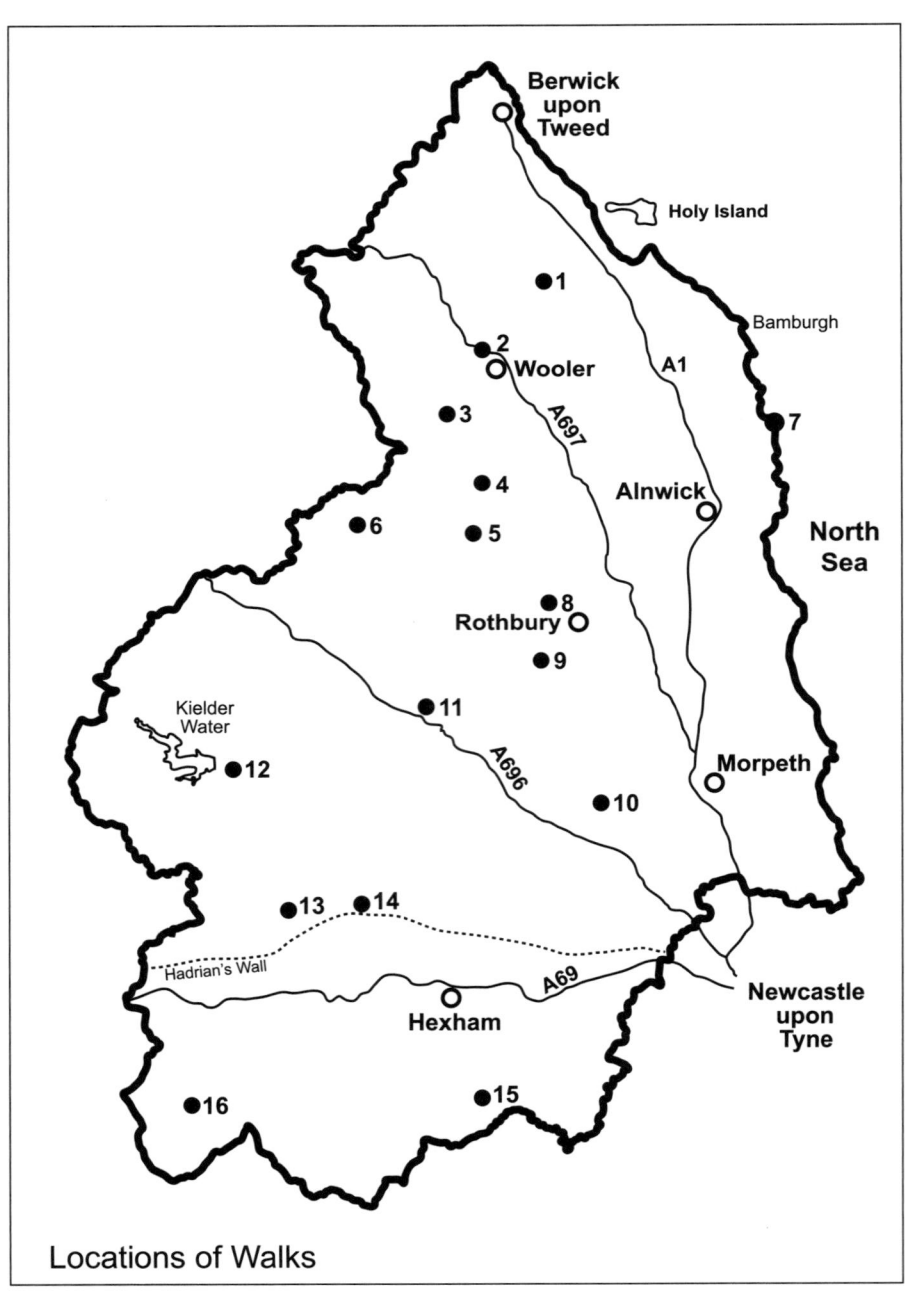

Locations of Walks

# Contents

**Introduction** — 7

1. **St Cuthbert's Cave and Swinhoe** — 9
   High Road 8.7 miles (14 kms) Low Road 7.1 miles (11.4 kms)

2. **Wooler and Humbleton Hill** — 15
   High Road 5.3 miles (8.5 km) Low Road using First Split Point 4 miles (6.4 km), or Second Split Point 4.7 miles (7.6 kms)

3. **Harthope Valley and Happy Valley** — 23
   High Road 6.2 miles (9.8 kms) Low Road 4.3 miles (6.9 kms)

4. **Breamish Valley: Wether Hill and Brough Law** — 31
   High Road 4.9 (7.8 kms) Low Road 4.6 miles (7.4 kms)

5. **Alnham and the Shepherds' Memorial Stone** — 38
   High Road 6.5 miles (10.5 kms) Low Road 5.4 miles (8.7 kms)

6. **Coquet Valley: Windy Gyle and the Scottish Border** — 45
   High Road 8.4 miles (13.5 kms) Low Road 7.4 miles (11.9 kms)

7. **The Northumberland Coast:** — 53
   **Low Newton to Craster and Howick**
   High Road 11.8 miles (13.9 kms) Low Road 7.7 miles (12.4 kms)

8. **Rothbury: Blaeberry Hill and Carriage Drives** — 61
   High Road 6.5 miles (10.5 kms) Low Road 6.1 miles (9.8 kms)

9. **Simonside Ridge and Spylaw** — 68
   High Road 6.5 miles (10 km) Low Road 4.5 miles (7.2 km) or 4.7 miles (7.6 km) with the detour to Church Rock

10. **Bolam Lake and Shaftoe Crags** — 76
    High Road 8.9 miles (14.3 kms) Low Road 7.6 miles (12.2 kms)

| 11. | **Elsdon and Landshot Hill** | 84 |
|---|---|---|
| | High Road 6 miles (9.7km) Low Road 4miles (6.4km) | |
| 12. | **Kielder Water: Leaplish to Tower Knowe** | 90 |
| | High Road 7.5 miles (12 km) Low Road 4.5 miles (7 km) | |
| 13. | **Hadrian's Wall and Greenlee Lough** | 96 |
| | High Road 7.7 miles (12.4 kms) Low Road 6 miles (9.6 kms) to Steel Rigg, where you can wait for the car, or 7.5 miles (12 kms) for the full distance back to the start point | |
| 14. | **Hadrian's Wall: Housesteads to Cawfields and Walltown** | 103 |
| | High Road 8.9 miles (14.3 kms) Low Road 6.2 miles (10 kms) | |
| 15. | **Blanchland and the Carriers' Way** | 111 |
| | High Road 9.5 miles (15.3 km) Low Road 6.5 miles (10.5 km) | |
| 16. | **South Tyne Trail and the Pennine Way** | 120 |
| | High Road 6.3 miles (10.1km) Low Road 4.9 miles (7.9 kms) | |

Anne Leuchars and Debby Waldron met while working in Newcastle and have walked many miles together since. They both live in Northumberland – Anne in the Tyne Valley, Debby in the north of the county.

Anne is a journalist, and she has also worked for the Northumberland National Park Authority. She has a lifelong love of the countryside and walking, and is very partial to a nice long rest on a wayside bench.

Debby works as a camera journalist. As well as exploring Northumberland she has ascended most of the Lake District Peaks before starting on Scotland's Munros. A keen traveller, she's also been to the summits of Kilimanjaro and Kinabalu, as well as trekking to Everest Base Camp, walking the Inca and Ausangate Trails in Peru and the Torres Del Paine Circuit in Patagonia.

# Introduction

This book proves that the tortoise and the hare can set off and finish at the same time, and enjoy each other's company along the way. It solves the problem of finding a walk which suits everybody in the family or group. Anne is the tortoise, a slow walker who likes to stop for a breather, and Debby is the hare, fit enough for any outdoor challenge. Together they have devised walks which bring equal pleasure to both types of walker.

## The Walks
Although there are 16 walks listed, there are in fact 32 in the book. Each chapter can be treated like a conventional walks guide, you simply have to choose which version to follow.

However, if you are a mixed ability group or couple, one of you can take the High Road and the other the Low Road. Each walk splits into harder routes for fitter people and easier tracks for slower, less sure-footed people. In most cases you all set off together, then separate part way through and meet up again at a clear rendezvous point to complete the walk together. For example the walks are suitable for families where perhaps grandparents could take young children on the easier route, leaving parents to stretch their legs over more challenging terrain. Or simply – as in Anne and Debby's case – where there is a difference in fitness levels.

The walks also accommodate differences in approach to a day in the countryside – some people like to stroll along and relish the views, taking advantage of benches or other rest points along the way. Others prefer a physical workout and the satisfaction of several miles or a steep hill conquered.

## The Countryside
Northumberland has it all. High rounded hills, long sandy beaches, castles, caves, hillforts, heather moorland, woodland, waterfalls...the list is long and lovely. Within the county are a World Heritage Site, a National Park and a Dark Sky Park. Such a wide variety of scenery offers countless walks to suit every mood and season.

The routes in this book sample many of the contrasting choices, and each requires several hours or a full day to complete. Even the easier Low Road options need some fitness and experience of country walking.

Underfoot, the walks vary from smooth surfaced tracks to boggy moorland. Most are well-signposted, but any landscape can change over time and no walking guide is a permanently accurate description of an area.

## Safety Tips

Some of the routes head into remote areas where there is no mobile phone signal, sparse habitations and few other walkers to help in an emergency. Proper walking boots and warm waterproof clothing are essential, as is an Ordnance Survey map – the sketch maps in this book are for general guidance only.

## Key to Maps

① ② ③ etc.   Walking together/High Road
Ⓐ Ⓑ Ⓒ etc.   Low Road routes
▲                    Trig Point or Cairn
🌲 🌲              Plantation or forest
〜                River or waterfall
■                    Buildings
Ⓡ                    Rendevous point

# Walk 1
# St Cuthbert's Cave and Swinhoe

*Both routes are on obvious, well-signposted tracks and paths, with gentle gradients. Each walk delivers a variety of scenery with the bonus of views of the sea and Holy Island.*

| Distances | High Road 8.7 miles (14 kms) <br> Low Road 7.1 miles (11.4 kms) |
|---|---|
| Duration | Approximately 4 hours |
| Parking | Free car park at Holburn Grange Farm (nearest sat nav postcode TD15 2UL). Look out for the faded National Trust sign pointing off the Chatton to Holburn road 0.6 mile (1 km) south of Holborn or 4.6 miles (7.4 kms) north of Chatton. Drive along the farm lane, turn left at the end to reach the car park at the end of a row of cottages. <br> Grid reference NU 051351 |
| Map | Ordnance Survey Explorer 340 'Holy Island & Bamburgh' |

## Walking Together

Leave the car park and turn left up the wide track between two hedges to reach a gate and a stile. As directed by the signpost for St Cuthbert's Cave, turn right and enjoy the springy grass of an inviting path.

1. When you reach a wooden gate and stile, with the St Cuthbert's Way sign, go through the gate to walk along a tree-lined avenue for a short distance until you see a path on your left leading up to St Cuthbert's Cave. It's well worth the short detour up to the cave.

   *In the 7th century Cuthbert ran the monastery on Holy Island, and travelled extensively as a bishop. He travelled even more after he*

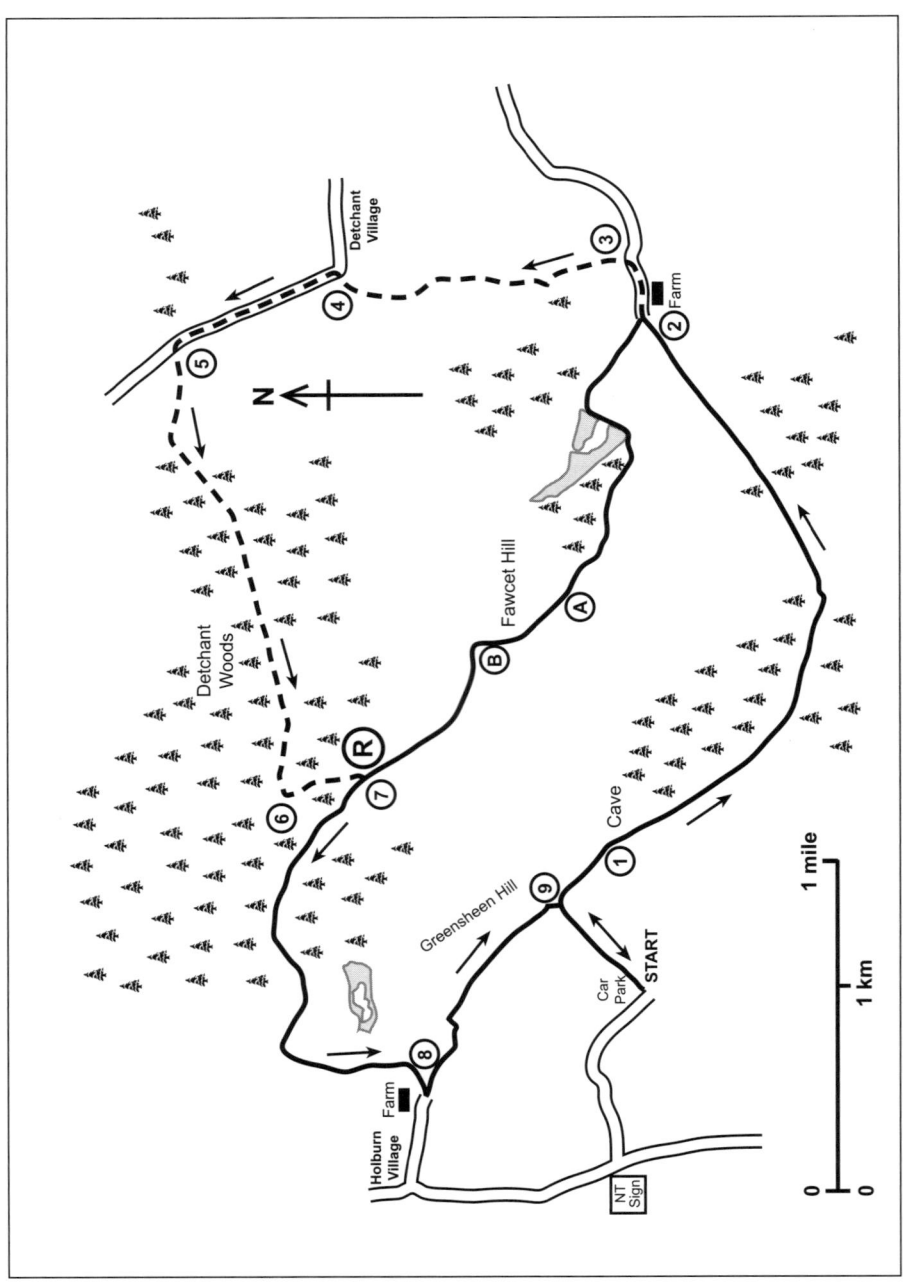

*died – his body was carried by monks all around northern England, reputedly resting for a while in this cave.*

After exploring the cave return to the main path and turn left, with a wide view of the whole Cheviot range on your right, from the Scottish Border to Simonside. Go through a wooden gate and stay on the track alongside the wood.

*You pass dramatic crags of sandstone, huge buttresses shaped and sculpted by winds, rain and frost.*

The track bears left into the woods, and you pass through a wooden gate with a notice requesting that dogs are kept on leads, and then a metal gate with a blue waymarker pointing straight on. The track develops into a farm lane.

2. When you reach the many buildings and barns of Swinhoe Farm the route descends to a junction of tracks. This is where the group splits up.

## High Road

Walk straight ahead along the road past a row of cottages on your right and farm buildings on your left. Just beyond the final outbuildings, look out for a public bridleway on the left, signposted 'Detchant 1 Mile'. Take this path.

3. Go over a burn and then through a metal gate. Continue through the field with a fence on your right. At the end of the field, go through another gate and turn sharp right through a second gate following the bridleway signs.

   Continue through the next field heading for a five-bar gate just in front of low farm buildings. Cross the fence via a stile and continue past a range of farm buildings to the end of the farm's private road.

4. At the end of this driveway, you come to a gate onto a minor road. Go through the gate and turn right towards the small village of Detchant. Walk past the first couple of houses and then turn left onto another country road, following a cycle-way signpost. Walk past 'Grans Cottage' and head down the quiet country lane.

St Cuthbert's Cave

*This is a lovely section of the walk – although you are walking on tarmac, you are unlikely to encounter any traffic. On your right are superb views towards Holy Island and the beautiful north Northumberland coastline.*

Cross the Kettle Burn by way of a stone bridge and continue straight ahead.

5. When you reach trees on your left opposite a small stone cottage, turn left into Detchant Woods, following a footpath sign towards Detchant Wood and Lowick.

After roughly ⅓ of a mile the path splits – stay left, on the main broad track, following a yellow footpath waymarker.

When you reach Ivy House, the path bears right. Continue to follow the main wide track through the trees.

6. At a major junction of paths, marked by a three-way fingerpost, leave the main track (which swings right). Instead, continue straight ahead, towards Greymare Farm and Swinhoe. This is a delightful broad grassy path which climbs steadily uphill through trees.

   When you reach a T-Junction of paths at the top of the hill, turn left onto St Cuthbert's Way, heading towards Greymare Farm.

7. At the next T-Junction of paths you should meet up with the rest of your party.

## Low Road

2. At the split point turn left in the direction of the fingerpost pointing to Holburn and Fenwick, with the blue logo of the St Oswald's Way. Walk up the farm track and as it rises and bears left you pass Upper Swinhoe Lake, a wonderfully peaceful stretch of water surrounded by trees. You can afford a short stop to enjoy the scene and listen to the coots and moorhens, before continuing along the track. This passes Lower Swinhoe Lake but the water is screened by trees.

A. After gradually ascending through Virgin Hill Wood a steel gate lets you out into open country. Walk alongside the dramatic crags of Fawcet Hill, studded with gorse.

   *To your left is the grassy vale of the Middleton Burn. The mounds and dips you can see are the remains of bell pits where coal was mined two centuries ago. Miners would sink a shaft and descend to dig around the base of the shaft in all directions until the pit in cross-section resembled the shape of a bell. Mining continued until the cavity became too dangerous and collapsed, and another mine was started nearby.*

   As the path curves to the right the crags disappear, leaving a stunning view of the sea and Holy Island with Lindisfarne Castle. On a clear day you can see the whole of Budle Bay, Bamburgh Castle to the south, and the Farne Islands.

B. Go through a gate and turn left on the public bridleway signposted Holburn. You are now on St Oswald's Way and St Cuthbert's Way. If you can bear to turn your back on the sea views, walk along the track, passing a small lake with a cabin on your right.

Staying on the main track, go through a gate to reach the edge of the forest. Go through another gate and a few yards along you reach the rendezvous point – a T-junction of forest tracks with a finger post. The High Road party will arrive from the Fenwick direction to the right.

## Walking Together
7. Take the bridleway signed 'Holburn 1¾ miles'. The path continues through the woods, soon skirting a wooden gate and heading gently downhill.

   *On your left is Holburn Lake and Holburn Moss Nature Reserve. The area is a Site of Special Scientific Interest for two main features: wild birds and the habitat. It's a peat bog and raised mire – these are rare in Britain and few remain intact. The lake and surrounding area are of international importance as a major roost for greylag geese and wildfowl. More than 2,000 geese have been counted here, representing more than 2% of the estimated north-west European population.*

   After the track curves alongside a stone-walled enclosure of trees on your right, go through a five-bar gate with a bridleway sign and continue straight ahead.

8. At the end of this section of track, and before you reach farm buildings, look out for a metal gate on your left. (There is a way-marker but you might only spot it once you are beyond it – however if you reach the farm you've gone too far). Go through the metal gate and continue in the direction of the way-marker along a grassy path.

   Go through a wooden gate and continue with a fence on your right and craggy Greensheen Hill up on your left.

9. After just over half a mile of walking from the farm, you reach a wooden gate and stile on your right. You will recognise this as the route back to the car park, so cross the stile and head down the broad track to return to your car.

# Walk 2
# Wooler and Humbleton Hill

*You leave the town of Wooler to reach open country, and the summit of Humbleton Hill. Your rewards for the steep climb are superb views and a sense of history – the Iron Age, a bloody battle against the Scots, and the lands where Borders Reivers exerted their violent tyranny. There are two options for the easier route: one retraces the outward trip, or a slightly longer return route goes back to the town via a quiet lane. The High Road route has a final section crossing Wooler Common through woodland.*

| Distances | High Road 5.3 miles (8.5 km)<br>Low Road using First Split Point is 4 miles (6.4 km), or Second Split Point is 4.7 miles (7.6 km) |
|---|---|
| Duration | Approximately 3½ hours |
| Parking | Wooler Bus Station car park on the High Street (nearest sat nav postcode NE71 6BY), pay and display, toilets. Grid reference NT 991280 |
| Map | Ordnance Survey Explorer OL 16 'The Cheviot Hills' |

## Walking Together

Exit the car park and turn right along the High Street, then go left onto Burnhouse Road. As you leave the town, Humbleton Hill is ahead of you behind the campsite. Walk past the entrance to the campsite and after crossing the road bridge, look for a wooden public footpath sign on your left signposted Humbleton.

1. Go through the little gate and walk up across the field. At the end of the field, go through another small gate and along a path to reach a lane.

2. Turn left and walk uphill to pass through the tiny hamlet of Humbleton.

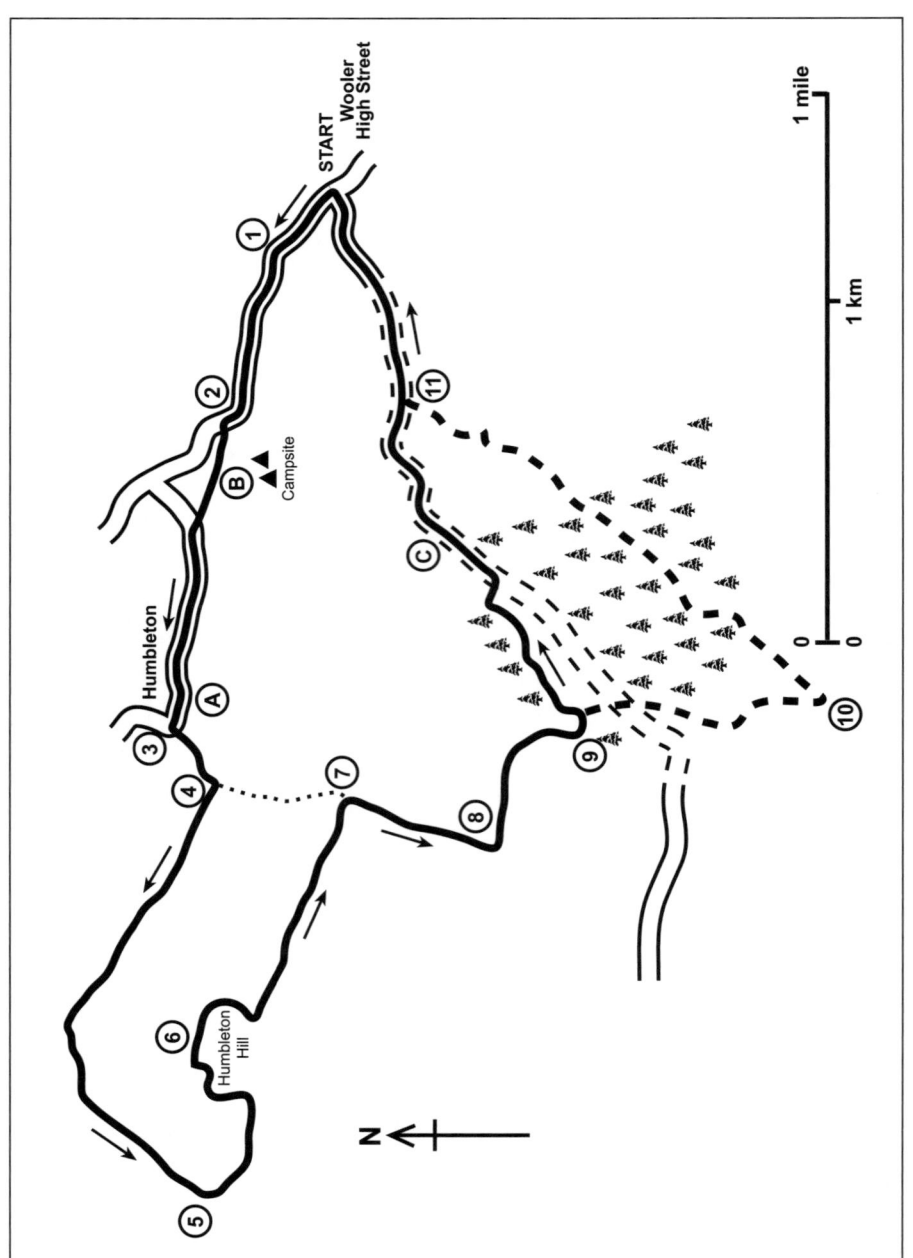

*Early spelling has it as Humbledown or Homildon, and Shakespeare called it Holmedon in Henry IV Part 1 (act 1 scene 1) as the battle and conquest of the Scots is reported.*

3. At the T-Junction and phone box, turn left up the lane with a road sign indicating no through road with no vehicle access.

4. Go through a wicket gate beside a six-bar gate and then turn right at a fingerpost 'Public Bridleway, Gleadscleugh'. Go over a stile beside another gate and follow signs for the Hillfort Trail. Walk straight on, along a lovely broad grassy path, with old mill ponds to your right and Humbleton Hill rising up on your left. Where the track forks beyond the ponds, take the left path, still following the Hillfort Trail. Go over a stile beside a gate and continue on the broad green path.

   *You might see gliders overhead from the Borders Gliding Club based at Milfield. The hillforts of this area are particularly spectacular when viewed from the air. Below you is the Milfield Plain, a rich agricultural area with fertile soils deposited by a prehistoric lake.*

   Keep following the trail as it heads steadily up and round to the left of the hill.

5. When you reach a junction of paths near a gate, and the main path appears to continue straight on, you need to turn off left, still following the Hillfort Trail sign. Cross a stile over a fence and continue on up.

   *As you climb steadily towards the summit, more hills come into view. Over to your right is the unmistakable whale-back shape of Cheviot, Northumberland's highest hill; behind you is Yeavering Bell, site of the county's largest Iron Age hillfort.*

   As you approach the summit you cross the remains of ramparts to reach the top of the hill and an impressive cairn.

   *It takes a bit of imagination to picture, but the hillfort would have been surrounded by a massive stone wall with a second inner wall protecting a group of round timber huts. It was first built in around 300BC.*

Take some time to enjoy the 360 degree views – to the east you can see the Northumberland coastline, to the west the Cheviot Hills, south of the hill is Wooler, and the northern views have the River Glen meandering through farmland to meet the River Till.

*Humbleton Hill was the site of a battle between the Scots and the English in 1402. The English were led by Harry "Hotspur" Percy, the eldest son of the Earl of Northumberland, while around 10,000 Scots had been assembled by the Earl of Douglas. English longbow archers gained the first advantage and in the fierce fighting that followed hundreds of Scots died, leaving Harry Hotspur victorious.*

6. From the summit cairn, re-trace your steps a few yards until you see a clear path heading down to your left, on the Wooler side of the hill. This steep grassy track takes you down to a five-bar gate.

7. The gate marks the point where the group will split if the Low Roaders are taking the shortest option and retracing the outward

Humbleton Hill

route from Wooler – see First Split Point below. Or Low Roaders can continue on to the Second Split Point.

## High Road

7. Pass through the gate at the bottom of Humbleton Hill and turn right onto the track. Continue on uphill, go through a gate and almost immediately, turn sharp left and pass through another five-bar gate.

8. Follow the lovely grassy track downhill towards woodland on the edge of Wooler Common. Go through the gate on the edge of the trees and walk down through the woods, following the St Cuthbert's Way marker posts.

9. When you reach a narrow tarmac track this is the Second Split Point, the alternative location for the group to split up.

   High Roaders turn right and cross the Humbleton Burn by the bridge which takes you into the car-park.

   *The information board is dedicated to 'Sheila' – a collie dog awarded an animal gallantry medal for helping to rescue four American airmen when their plane crashed on the Cheviot in December 1944.*

   Head for the road, turn right and then almost immediately left onto a public bridleway signposted St Cuthbert's Way. Cross the fence using a stone stepped stile and continue on the path uphill ahead of you. The path climbs steadily through bracken before emerging onto the open hillside. Shortly after that, the path forks. Take the left-hand fork, heading towards a conifer plantation with a gate and fence at its corner.

   *If you pause at the gate and look back you'll see how Humbleton Hill dominates the area and can appreciate why our Iron Age ancestors chose to build a fort there. It's one of a series of hillforts around the fringes of the Cheviot Hills – more can be explored in Walk 4 in the Breamish Valley.*

10. Go through the gate and follow the St Cuthbert's Way through the trees. The path winds through the plantation before emerging at a

Humbleton Hill view

gate onto open land above Wooler. Where a small dirt track crosses your path, ignore it and continue straight on ahead, downhill on the broad grassy track. This leads you to a wicket gate. Go through this and follow the gravel lane in front of a red-roofed cottage.

11. This track leads down to a tarmac road and houses. Turn right and follow the road back into the centre of Wooler, where you will rendezvous with the rest of your group.

## Low Road

**Split Point 1** – Go through the gate at the base of Humbleton Hill (point 7 on the map) and turn left onto the stony track, with the hill high above you on the left. Soon you pass the bridleway signpost that took you towards the ponds on your outward journey.

A. From here you pass the cottage with a red-tiled roof and retrace your steps through the hamlet of Humbleton.

B. You'll recognise where you turn off the lane, signposted 'Public Footpath Burnhouse Road ¼ mile', so you follow the short footpath, go down the field to the road, and turn right to return to Wooler past the campsite entrance.

*You're probably slightly ahead of the High Roaders so you might like to pop into the Tourist Information Centre set back from Burnhouse Road in Padgepool Place, beside the Cheviot Primary Care Centre.*

**Split Point 2** is the longer Low Road route – At the narrow tarmac track near the Forestry Commission car park (point 9 on the map) turn left.

*This track has more benches per yard than any other path in this book. You should have time to try out one of them for a few minutes and also to study the many information panels with details of the surrounding trees and wildlife*

As you pass a pond on your right the tarmac track with side rails bends right but you go straight on along a grassy path beside the trees. Follow the path as it veers right, alongside a fence, to reach an unsurfaced driveway. Turn right up the slope to the road.

C. Go left onto Common Road, and after you pass High Fair on your left you'll see a lane coming in from the right. This is where your companions will be re-joining your route, but unless you happen to coincide with them, it's simpler to meet back in Wooler. Continue down Ramsey's Lane into the Market Place and turn left onto the High Street.

# Walk 3
# Harthope Valley and Happy Valley

*Both routes take you through scenery to make your heart sing. The longer walk follows the Harthope Burn before taking you up into the hills on wide grassy tracks where the views just get better and better. The shorter route favours the Coldgate Water (same river, different name) using a narrow path traversing the valley side followed by a high level grassy track through the remnants of ancient settlements. You return together as happy walkers via Happy Valley.*

| Distances | High Road: 6.2 miles (9.8 kms)<br>Low Road: 4.3 miles (6.9 kms) |
|---|---|
| Duration | Approximately 3 hours 40 minutes |
| Parking | The nearest place name on the map is Middleton Hall, reached by leaving Wooler via Cheviot Street and going through Earle. At Middleton Hall turn right, signposted Langleeford and drive into the valley. At Skirl Naked (nearest sat nav postcode NE71 6RE) the road drops steeply and you park on the wide grass verge on the right just before Carey Burn Bridge, distinctive with its white railings.<br>Grid reference NT 976249 |
| Map | Ordnance Survey Explorer OL 16 'The Cheviot Hills' |

## Walking Together
Leave the car and turn right along the tarmac road to cross Carey Burn Bridge. You split up on the other side of the bridge.

## High Road
1. Continue along the road into the valley. You may prefer to walk on the wide grassy pasture, or haugh, at the side of the road – kinder

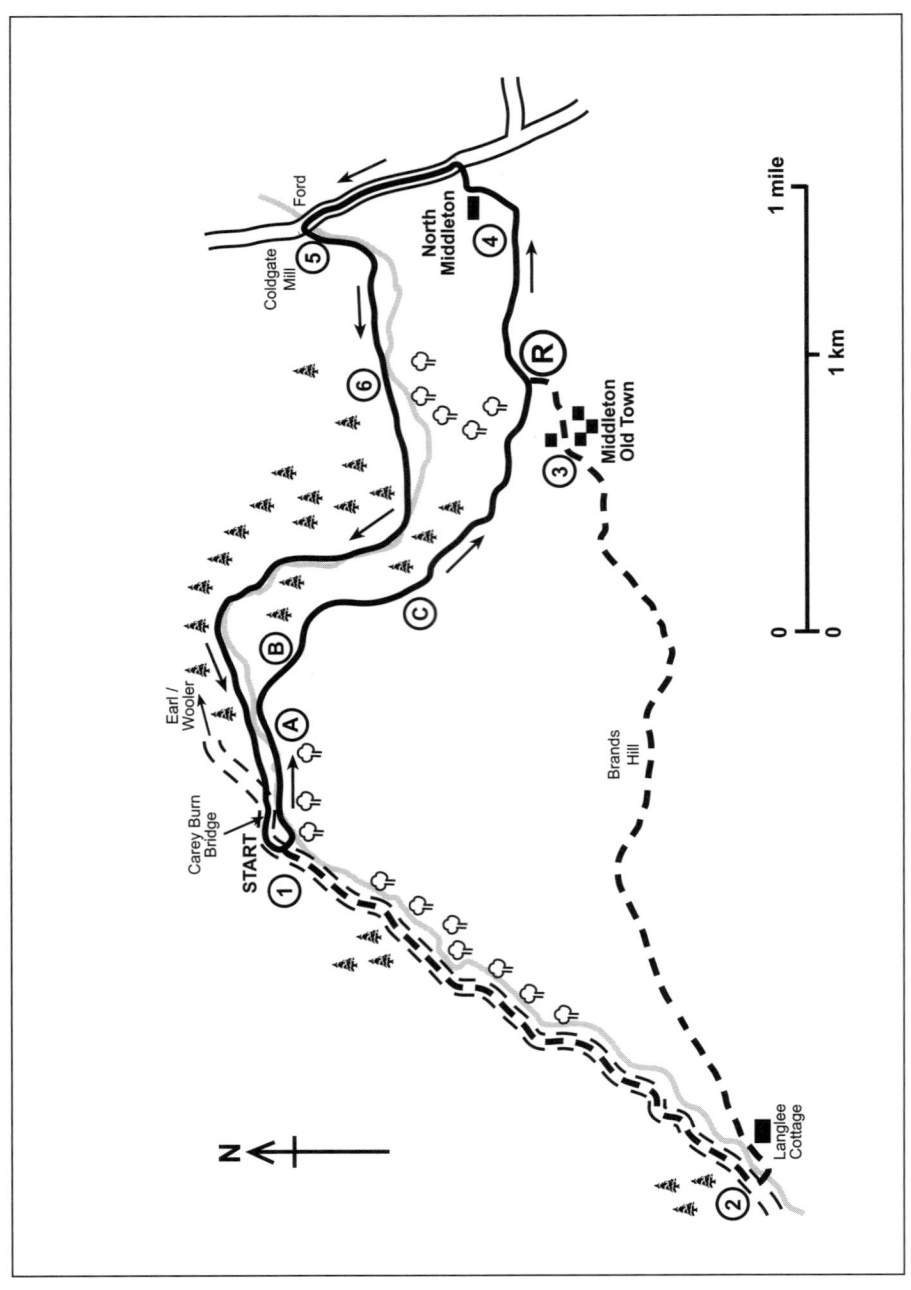

Rush hour in the Harthope Valley

on the feet than tarmac – beside the pretty Harthope Burn. After around a mile, cross a cattle grid and continue on along the valley.

*Ahead of you are Cheviot (on your right) and Hedgehope, the two highest hills in Northumberland at 2,343 feet (714 metres) and 2,674 feet (815 metres) respectively.*

Cross a little road bridge over the beautiful Backwood Burn. Soon after a cattle grid you will see a cottage to your left on the other side of the burn.

2. Just beyond this turn left off the road at the signpost to 'Middleton Old Town'. Go over the bridge and up the driveway towards Langlee Cottage. Pass to the left of the fence using the narrow path alongside the private garden.

Looking across the Harthope Valley

Once past the house, go through a gate and pick up a clear path. This is a lovely green, grassy track going on up the hill to your left at a steady climb.

When the path starts to level out towards the top of the hill, you reach a crossroads of paths. Go straight on, over the broad grass track and continue on up the hill towards a gate which you can see on the skyline ahead.

Cross the stile beside the gate. Carry on along the broad grassy track ahead of you, with a deep valley on your right hand side.

Cross another broad grassy track and keep heading downhill, aiming to the left of the sheep pens ahead of you. When you reach the fence, cross using the ladder stile.

Continue walking downhill with the fence on your right, cross another fence by a stile and continue straight ahead.

3. Ahead of you are the remains of a shepherd's cottage, long ago deserted. Continue downhill past the ruin.

*As you proceed, look to your right and you can just make out the remains of the hamlet of Middleton Old Town, a medieval village which was home to around a dozen people at one time. All that remains now are some stones, half-buried in the grass.*

As you follow the path round to the left you will reach a corner with a stile and waymarker. Turn left through the small gate and head down to the footbridge which is your rendezvous point.

## Low Road

1. After crossing Carey Burn Bridge immediately go left at the fingerpost for 'Middleton Old Hall', go through the small gate, turn right and cross the footbridge. Follow the narrow footpath up the valley side.

*The path is steep, narrow and slightly eroded in places but you are accompanied by the sound of the burn, widening views and a lovely mix of trees, some of them ancient and gnarled.*

A. When you see a corner of wooden and wire fences look for the waymarker with two arrows, one pointing slightly right and the other sharp right. Don't turn sharp right and up along the fence line, and don't go straight on along the well-trodden path, but head slightly right towards open country. This path is indistinct at first, but after a few yards it becomes clearer.

B. After crossing a small stream you turn right, uphill, with the burn on your right. Soon you pick up a clear track, and you'll see a post with a waymarker straight ahead of you. Follow the direction of the waymarker, straight up through clumps of gorse. Pass to the left of the fenced-in boggy spring and veer left to the next waymarker, then straight on along the grassy track with valley views below and heather moorland on Brands Hill above you.

*On either side of you are the remains of many ancient settlements and homesteads, evidence of continuous communities farming this land through the Bronze Age, the Iron Age and during the Roman occupation.*

C. The path ascends gently until it meets a stone wall with hawthorn trees where you'll see a marker post pointing to the left. Take this route directly downhill towards the conifer plantation, turning right at the waymarker on the broken fence. Stay on this wide track over stile beside a gate, and on to a second gate with a ruined building visible ahead. You cross the stile and turn left, down the field, with the wood on your left. After passing through a small gate you reach the footbridge rendezvous point.

## Walking Together
Walk up the short steep slope that the High Roaders came down, go through the small gate and straight on through another wooden gate and down the wide farm track. You'll soon see the extensive farm buildings of North Middleton on the left. Approach them by crossing a stile beside the steel gate to walk diagonally right across the field. Look for a steel gate on the left of the farm building with a rusty corrugated metal roof, go through this and turn right through the farmyard to reach the tarmac road. At the road, go left and follow it until you see a ford ahead of you, with a footbridge which will take you into woodland.

The Carey Burn

*Near here the river changes its name again. You have met it as the Harthope Burn and Coldgate Water. From now on it wishes to be known as Wooler Water.*

After crossing the stone bridge beside the ford, go through a kissing gate and turn left into the trees on a broad track. You are now walking in the lovely Happy Valley.

After a while you leave the trees behind and come onto a broad grassy plain. Keep going with the burn on your left. At the end of the field cross a stile beside a gate and continue on in the same direction.

Where a path forks off into the trees on the right heading sharply uphill, do not be tempted to follow it. Instead, look for a way-marker which indicates a path heading through the gorse, staying low with the burn still on your left. The path narrows here and goes back into woodland above the Carey Burn.

Where the field comes close to the road, look for a stile beside a gate on the roadside. Cross it, turn left, and return to your car.

## Walk 4
# Breamish Valley: Cochrane Pike and Brough Law

*There isn't much difference in the length of these two walks, but the High Road route has more uphill work and a steep descent, whereas the Low Road starts downhill sooner and has a more gentle descent. Both walks deliver superb views and a trip back in time – this area has a wealth of evidence of human activity spanning at least five millennia from the Neolithic to the post-medieval period.*

| Distances | High Road 4.9 (7.8 kms)<br>Low Road 4.6 miles (7.4 kms) |
|---|---|
| Duration | Approximately 3 hours |
| Parking | Bulby's Wood Car Park (nearest sat nav postcode NE66 4LT), free, toilets. Directions: Turn west off the A697 one mile north of Powburn and follow the road along the valley. The car park is on the right, half a mile after Ingram Farm and cottages. Grid reference NT 007164 |
| Map | Ordnance Survey Explorer OL 16 'The Cheviot Hills' |

## Walking Together
From the car park turn left and walk along the tarmac lane, cross a cattle grid and pass a row of cottages.

1. Where the lane bends left you go straight on, signposted 'Ingram Mill ½', passing a group of holiday cottages.

2. When you see Ingram Village Hall ahead of you turn right at a fingerpost pointing to Prendwick, go through a wooden gate and

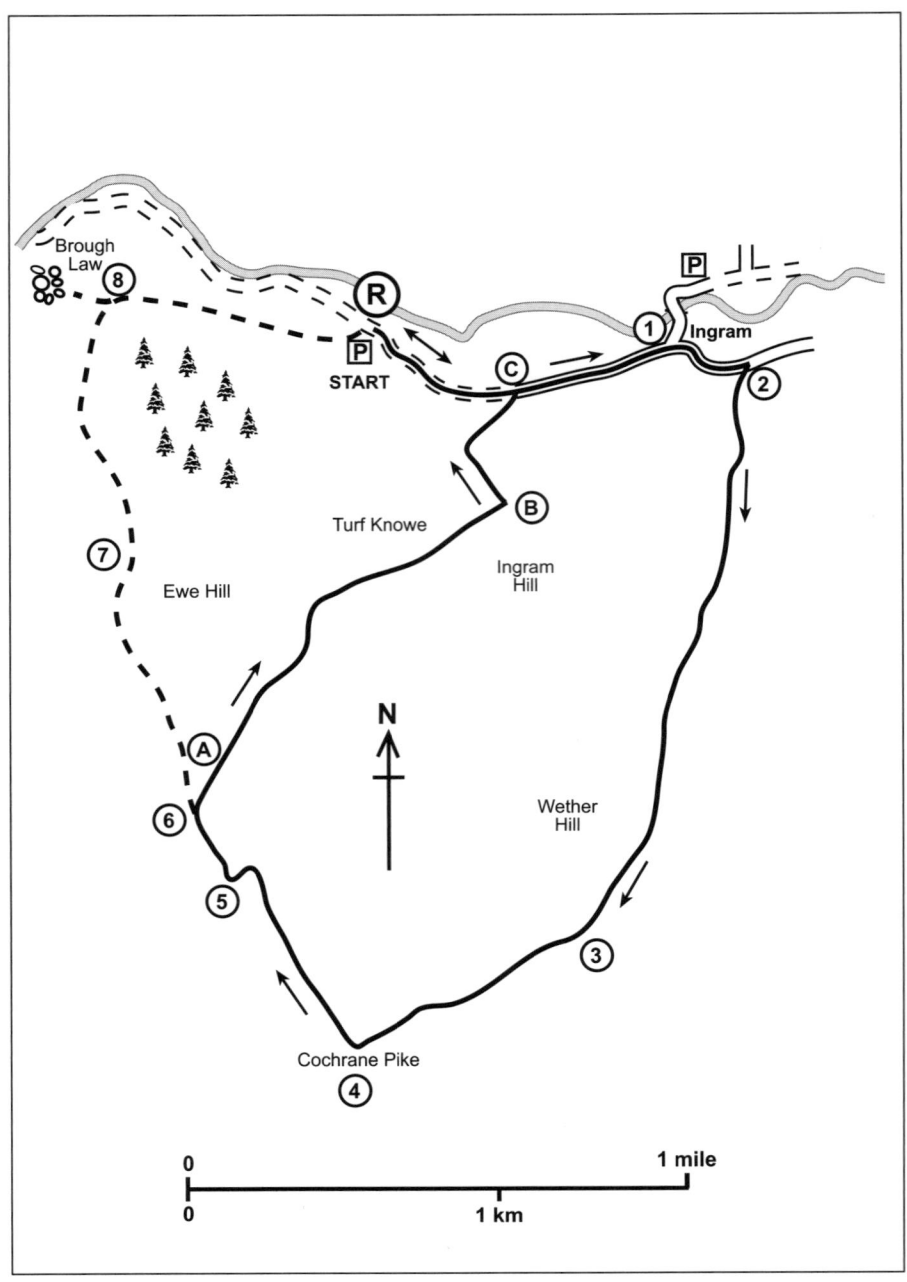

uphill on a stony track. At the next gate and stile the track bends right and you continue to follow it uphill as the views expand around you. After passing through a steel gate the track becomes grassy, taking you to a wooden gate and stile. The track is now stony again and it curves around to the right, skirting Wether Hill.

3. You ascend gradually and eventually a waymarker comes into view on the horizon. When you reach it take the right hand fork onto a grassy uphill path. You are now between Wether Hill on the right and Cochrane Pike on the left.

*Your destination is Cochrane Pike, but it's worth a quick detour up Wether Hill on your right to see the clear remains of the Iron Age hillfort with its double ramparts which would have enclosed around twenty timber roundhouses. Archaeologists have discovered that the hill was also used in Neolithic and Bronze Age times for burials. Retrace your steps to rejoin the main route.*

Breamish Valley (hillfort trail)

Walk up a wide grassy path onto Cochrane Pike. Occasional Hillfort Trail waymarkers guide you to the summit where there are views in all directions, taking in the Simonside Hills and the Cheviots.

*The defences and house remains are less distinct on Cochrane Pike, but you might be able to pick out the line of a dyke between your viewpoint and Wether Hill, possibly a boundary between the territories of the two communities.*

4. At the waymarker post on the summit of Cochrane Pike you turn hard right to continue along the Hillfort Trail. The path drops fairly steeply, heading towards a deep gully with a deciduous plantation beyond it.

*On the right you can see distinctive parallel lines in the landscape – these are cultivation terraces formed as farmers ploughed along the contours. Throughout the Breamish Valley there are various examples of these, both running horizontally around the curves of the land and tracking vertically up and down the hills, dating from the Iron Age to Medieval times. Grains such as barley and oats would have been grown.*

Cross a stile to descend into the gully, then there's a steep climb out again and you turn left at the top, along the fence line.

5. At the corner of the fence turn right (don't go through the little gate) and with the fence on your right walk gradually uphill.

6. You will reach a junction of tracks with a gate and stile on the right. Here your group will split up.

## High Road
6. Go straight on up the hill on the grassy path, still following the Hillfort Trail green markers, initially with the post and wire fence on your right. Where you reach the corner of the fenced area keep straight ahead, bearing slightly round to the right following the contours of the hill.

After a short gentle downhill section you reach a T-Junction. Turn right here, following the waymarker.

View from the top of Brough Law

After a couple of minutes there is an intersection of paths – turn left here, heading along the crest of the hill with a plantation down to your left and beyond it a view of the road wiggling along the valley all the way to Hartside. The hill with the knobbles on its summit is Hartside Hill.

Around half a mile from that last junction you reach Brough Law, its summit marked by large pile of stones.

*The hillfort was defended by massive stone walls and dramatic ramparts. When the remains of hut circles were excavated Roman pottery was found and also a 5th or 6th century knife, suggesting the site was occupied long after its Iron Age origins. The residents had views in all directions – you can pretty well see the whole of the Breamish Valley and surrounding hills.*

From the summit, re-trace your steps to an obvious path which skirts round to the left of the plantation. Follow the broad grass path down the hill – it is steep, but good underfoot. Turn left just before the bottom of the hill to reach your car.

## Low Road
6. Turn right, over the stile, following Public Bridleway signs and head down the grassy track with the plantation to your right.

A. After another gate and stile you continue gradually downhill on a wide track. Straight ahead you can see Reaveley Hill with its distinctive cultivation terraces. Ignore other paths and tracks which meet your main route and continue downhill.

*As you enjoy the solitude and a blissful 'away from it all' feeling, a glance at the Ordnance Survey map will show you how busy these hills were in the past. Surrounding you in all directions are cultivation terraces, settlements, enclosures, hillforts and burial cairns – reminders of the days when the Cheviots were much more heavily populated than today.*

B. The grassy track becomes a stony road and as it swings left you will see Brough Law ahead of you with a conifer plantation on its flank – this is where your High Road colleagues are.

C. The track eventually meets the tarmac lane; you turn left onto the lane and back to the car park.

# Walk 5
# Alnham and the Shepherds' Memorial Stone

*These two routes take you high enough for great views, and far enough into the hills to be totally surrounded by their undulating crests. On a beautiful day they bring great joy, but they hold a reminder of tragedy as you pass a memorial to two shepherds who died in a blizzard. The walks follow farm tracks and grassy paths, with a few indistinct sections and boggy patches.*

| Distances | High Road 6.5 miles (10.5 kms)<br>Low Road 5.4 miles (8.7 kms) |
|---|---|
| Duration | Approximately 4½ hours |
| Parking | Park on the wide grass verge outside Alnham Church (nearest sat nav postcode NE66 4TL). From the south the approach is via Thropton and Netherton, from the east or north leave the A697 at Whittingham and head west. Grid reference NT 991109 |
| Map | Ordnance Survey Explorer OL 16 'The Cheviot Hills' |

## Walking Together
Walk along the road with the church on your right. Pass the former vicarage with its fortified pele tower, built as protection from raids by the Border Reivers. Turn right just after the pele tower, along a path signposted 'Shank House and Low Bleakhope'.

Go through a gate into a meadow and head uphill, keeping to the left alongside a wall and heading toward a clump of conifers. Go through another two gates, still ascending and gaining ever-wider views. You are following purple waymarkers labelled 'restricted byway'. Pass a deciduous wood on your left, where the path can be wet and muddy, and continue uphill with a wall on your left.

1. As you reach open country you go through a wicket gate and bear right, still following the purple arrows. Head towards a hummock with large exposed stones on it and you'll see the path skirting to the left of it. Ahead is a single post waymarker at the wide stony track, which you follow uphill for short distance.

2. As the scenery widens out wonderfully, look for a fingerpost at a right-hand bend in the track. Here you leave the stony track and go straight on along a grassy track, still following the purple waymarkers.

   *You are walking along the ancient Salter's Road, a packhorse track used to carry salt from the coast through Northumberland to Scotland during the medieval period. In the 17th and 18th centuries this was one of the major routes used by drovers who moved large herds of cattle up and down the country.*

   Surrounded by wide and beautiful scenery, you go gently downhill to cross the Coppath Burn, then up to a gate in the wall ahead. On the Ordnance Survey map this is marked 'White Gate'. It's not white.

3. Go over the ladder stile at the gate and head slightly right, still following the purple waymarkers. A steady ascent passes a circular stone sheepfold on your right, and soon you reach a crossroads of grassy tracks marked by a single, shin-high stone.

4. Turn left, follow the track and keep right at a fork, onto the inviting wide grassy route gradually ascending High Knowes.

   *As the track starts to descend you will see a big stone memorial to Jock Scott and Willie Middlemas, shepherds who died on High Knowes in a blizzard in November 1962. They were trying to get home to remote Ewartly Shank by tractor and it was two days before they were reported missing. Their deaths led to the founding of the Northumberland National Park Mountain Rescue Team.*

5. After visiting the memorial, return to the path and continue downhill to reach a narrow tarmac lane. This is where the group splits up.

The Shepherds' Memorial cairn

## High Road

5. Turn right onto the tarmac road and head for a five bar gate. Just before the gate and cattle grid, you will reach a fingerpost, signed to 'Biddlestone'. Turn onto the grass, following the direction of the post. Keeping left, you reach a waymarker post. There are several of these across the next section of ground, which can be wet. The marker posts are short and rather difficult to spot.

After around 15 minutes of walking you will reach a wicket gate in the fence ahead of you. Go through the gate, and continue towards a group of boulders. Do not be tempted to go downhill – skirt to the right of the boulders, then left beyond them: a path zig-zags down to the burn which can be crossed at a narrow point using stepping stones which might be slippery. A fairly clear path ascends to the left on the far bank.

6. You are now on the remains of Tod Stones farmstead – essentially a scattering of large stones.

   *A group of stone buildings on the north bank of the Spartley Burn has been excavated by archaeologists. One had a stone structure that might have been an illicit whisky still – one of many in these hills in the 17th and 18th centuries.*

   Pick your way through the stones aiming for a stile over the fence ahead of you. Cross the fence using the stile and turn sharp right, heading uphill towards a farm track (reached adjacent to a five bar gate).

7. Turn left onto the track, and skirt around the contours of the hill. Eventually, after coming right around the hill, you will see a small conifer plantation ahead of you, on the right, adjacent to the track.

8. When you reach the plantation, bear left. There is no clear path down to the burn so make your way across the rough pasture and bog grass into the valley of the Hazeltonrig Burn. It is important to head towards the right hand end of the long narrow plantation on the far bank: there is a stile into the wood about one-quarter of the distance along from the right-hand corner.

9. Head uphill on the far bank, find the stile and pass through the plantation. The track is indistinct and quite overgrown with branches but by heading diagonally right you will reach the exit stile over the far fence. Once you are out of the trees, turn left, looking out for a stile ahead of you. Walk straight across this field and the next, towards another plantation.

   *Conifer plantations have an atmosphere all of their own. Unlike mixed woodland, the darkness and uniformity of the trees can feel claustrophobic to some. But the silence of a plantation has a kind of magic - and they do offer shelter from bad weather. If you are not a fan of these "artificial" woods, be reassured that a more open landscape of hills awaits you on the other side!*

10. Enter this plantation via another stile, walk through it on the path, and exit in the corner over a stile into a large grassy field. From

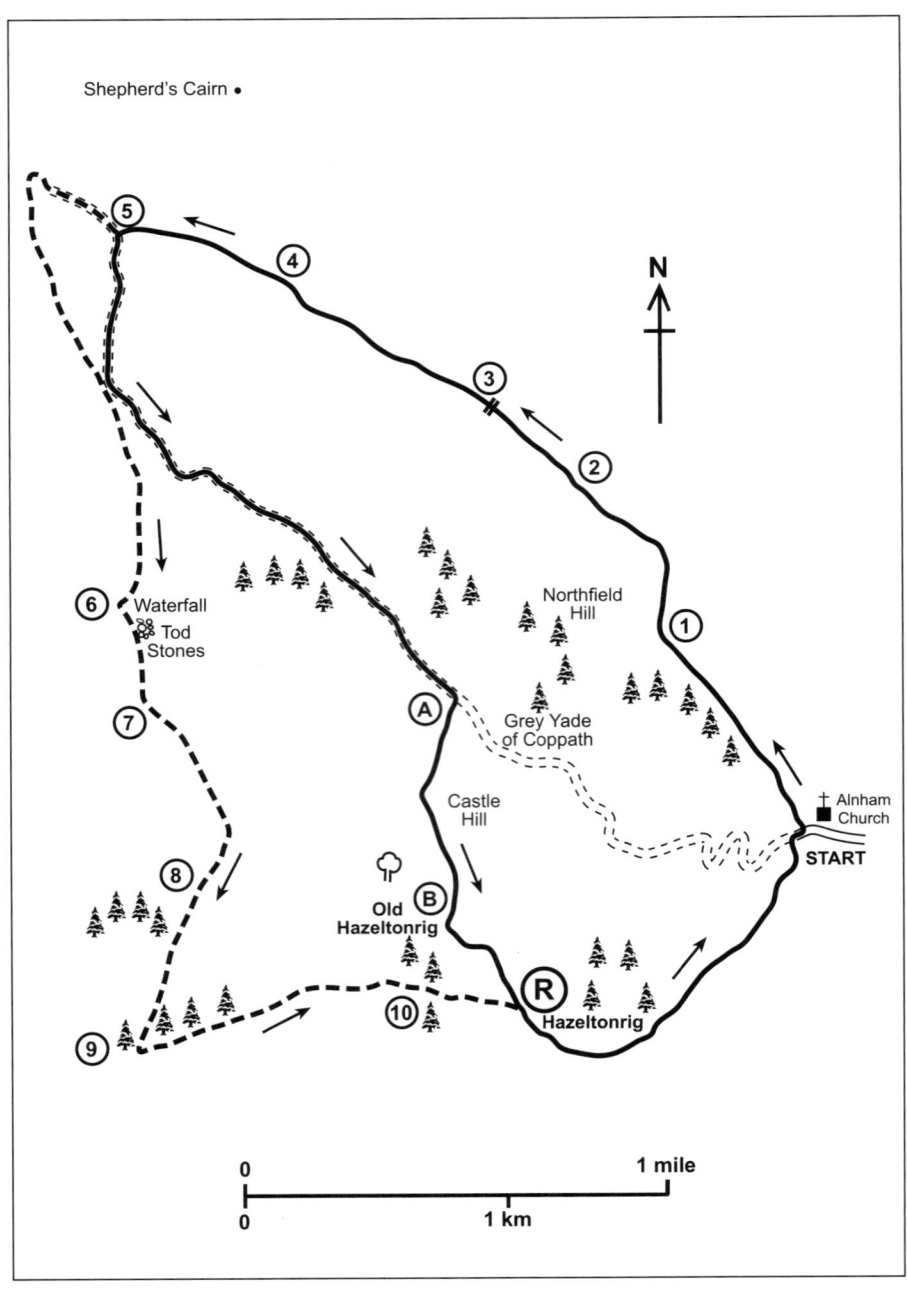

here, walk ahead, bearing half-right – you are aiming for the roof of a converted farm steading which should be visible beyond the trees ahead of you.

Descend, and cross over a red farm track to reach a wicket gate in the corner of the fence beside a wood – this is where you rendezvous with the other members of your group.

## Low Road

5. Turn left on the tarmac lane and walk downhill along the tarmac road.

*You are once again reminded of the fate of the two shepherds and wild winter weather of these hills when you see the tall metal posts which mark the roadside when snow blankets the land. The view ahead is filled with the Simonside Ridge.*

A. You leave the road just before it crosses the Coppath Burn. Turn right at a fingerpost marked 'Public Bridleway Old Hazelton Rig and Hazeltonrig', cross a small footbridge and walk up towards a gate. Go through the left hand wooden gate and follow the lovely grassy track with the sparkly Spartley Burn in the bottom of the steep valley. Don't be tempted by the obvious track down into the valley, but just past the waymarker aim slightly to the right of the farm buildings ahead.

*Looking down on you from across the valley is the Iron Age fort and settlement of Castle Hill dating from the second half of the first millennium BC. There are many hillforts in the Cheviot Hills, this one being distinctive for its multiple ramparts*

The track takes you down to the Hazeltonrig Burn, which you cross and follow the farm track up towards Old Hazeltonrig.

B. Go through a gate, turn left, and through another gate to the right of the buildings. Turn right and leave the farmyard along the track, following it downhill. When the track swings to the right, you go straight on over the grass to a stile and wicket gate in the corner on your left beside a wood. This is the rendezvous point.

## Walking Together

Go through the wicket gate and follow the grassy path downhill, with the trees on your left. Cross the footbridge and walk past the converted farm steading and small bungalow.

Ignore the footpath sign near the bungalow pointing into the plantation, and continue on for about 70 yards then turn left up the grassy track which climbs fairly steeply towards a gate.

Go through the gate, and keep on the track through two fields, heading half-left and steadily downhill. There are beautiful views all around you, including the tiny hamlet of Alnham off to your right.

Aim for the clump of trees that surrounds Alnham Church. By now, you should be able to see the church and indeed your car, so will know to turn right onto the tarmac lane, and over the cattle grid to regain your starting point.

## Walk 6
# Windy Gyle and the Scottish Border

*Windy Gyle is a very special place. You have to work hard to get there, which adds to the euphoric feeling as you stand at the top with England on one side of you and Scotland on the other. The views and the atmosphere are amazing. It's a steady ascent and steep descent along well-marked paths for both Low Roaders and High Roaders, but the Low Roaders do a shorter route by dropping off their fitter companions to start their walk from further away. This means a Low Roader needs to be the car driver.*

| Distances | High Road 8.4 miles (13.5 kms) <br> Low Road 7.4 miles (11.9 kms) |
|---|---|
| Duration | Approximately 5 hours |
| Parking | Drive up the Coquet Valley, passing Harbottle and Alwinton (there are toilets in the village car park) and drive on alongside the river for a further 5.5 miles, to reach Barrowburn (nearest sat nav postcode NE65 7BP). Stop at Wedder Leap car park and drop off the High Road walkers (refreshments available at Barrowburn Farm Tea Room, which has toilets for customers only). Low Roaders drive on up the valley for half a mile and park on the right just before the bridge at Trows Road End, distinctive with its white railings. Park on the grass behind the information board. Grid reference NT 859115 |
| Map | Ordnance Survey Explorer OL 16 'The Cheviot Hills' |

## High Road
From the drop-off point at Wedder Leap car park, turn left along the tarmac road. At the corner, where the road bends sharply left, turn right onto a footpath/bridleway marked 'Border Ridge'.

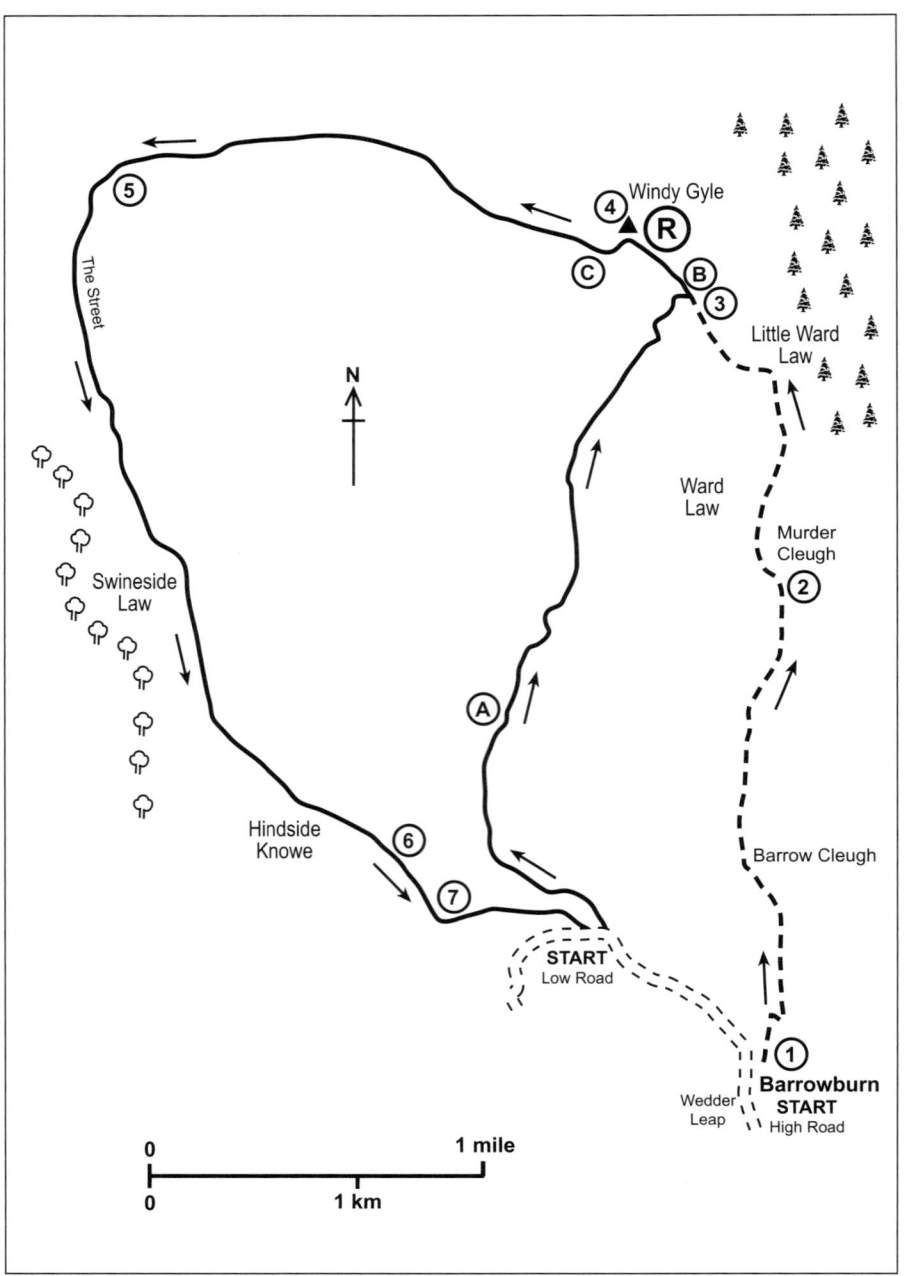

1. When you reach a waymarker post, turn left onto an uphill bridleway. You are now on the Border County Ride, a 100 mile circular route designed for horse riders. Walk along a broad, grassy track which climbs steadily uphill towards a five-bar gate. Go through the gate and continue your ascent.

   The walking here is usually excellent underfoot. The path climbs steadily before levelling out adjacent to Broad Law, with the Border Ridge (your eventual goal) ahead of you in the distance. After around 45-60 minutes walking, you reach a small plantation of trees with the rather menacing name of Murder Cleugh.

   *A stone nearby explains the name, as it commemorates an incident in 1610 when the landowner Robert Lumsden murdered his pregnant mistress.*

2. Go through a gate beside the plantation and turn right onto a broad gravel track.

Classic Cheviot views from Windy Gyle

*The Northumberland National Park Authority is planting native trees here, and already this sometimes rather bleak conifer-dominated landscape is being softened by their introduction.*

About 250 metres along the gravel track turn left up a farm track and through a gate marked with a sign prohibiting military vehicles. Follow the track as it winds steadily uphill, skirting round to the right of Ward Law.

The path goes through an area of what can be rather boggy ground before traversing Little Ward Law, and then dropping down towards a valley. If you look to your left here, you should be able to see another footpath. This is the route your Low Roaders are taking, so it's worth keeping a look-out for them from this point onwards.

3. When you reach the crest of a hill, the path bends around to the left quite sharply and you get to a three-way marker – pointing up to the summit, down towards the Low Roaders' route, and back the way you've just come. Carry on uphill in the direction of the Border Ridge.

4. When you reach a fingerpost pointing left and right, take the right-hand fork, which will lead you directly to the summit of Windy Gyle, via a stile over the fence which marks the Border. Once here, you cannot fail to miss the vast summit cairn.

*You are now officially in Scotland, making this a two-country walk! To your north, the Scottish Borders, to the south is Northumberland, and whichever direction you look in, you will see total wilderness and tranquillity (unless the army are using their big guns of course...)*

## Low Road

From the parking area walk with the Rowhope Burn on your left along the narrow tarmac lane (not the road you have been driving along beside the River Coquet, you want the lane heading north towards a cattle grid). Cross the grid and continue alongside the burn.

Don't worry about the sign 'Ministry of Defence Private Road No Unauthorised Access'. Almost a quarter of the Northumberland

National Park is owned by the Ministry of Defence and is used for military training, but this area is designated a 'dry training area' where there is no live firing and walkers are welcome. However, if military units are nearby you could hear loud explosions and gunfire.

A. After about half a mile you reach Rowhope farm, and less than half a mile beyond that is another farm, Trows, where there is a ford with two wooden footbridges. Leave the tarmac lane here and go left up the track and through the gate. Follow the clear track steeply uphill and after a second gate it becomes slightly less steep. Although it's quite a tough ascent you quickly gain views which take your breath away just as much as the effort of walking uphill. The broad grassy track narrows to a path as it climbs to reach a junction with a bridleway at a waymarker pointing in three directions.

B. You turn left and continue to head uphill.

Heading up the Border County Ride

*49*

*Your High Road companions will also be using this path so you might meet them here, although the official rendezvous point is further up.*

C. At the next waymarker take the path to the right and soon a gate comes into view, with a big mound of stones behind it. This is Russell's Cairn, the rendezvous point. You have walked into Scotland and reached an elevation of 2,030 feet (619 metres).

*Russell's Cairn is a Bronze Age burial site, but it got its name from a 16th century murder. Lord Francis Russell, who was responsible for security on the English side of the border, was allegedly killed here in 1585 during a supposed day of truce between the Scots and the English.*

## Walking Together

4. To leave the summit, return to the fingerpost near the stile and turn right, signposted 'Chew Green'. You are now walking on the Pennine Way.

   The path heads steeply downhill before reaching a stile beside a gate. Carry on downhill, enjoying the stunning views on either side.

   Along the fence line, you may notice some stars on metal posts. These mark objects of historical or archaeological importance which are buried underground, so that they don't get damaged during military manoeuvres.

   Head away from the fence now and continue on the clear path, heading mainly downhill but with a few ups as well.

5. After 1½ miles you reach a junction of paths, at which you need to turn left onto 'The Street'.

   *This is an ancient drovers' road, one of many in this area of the Borders. General Roy's military map of 1775 called this "the clattering road" - perhaps a reference to the sound of hooves on stony ground. Today it is a far greener and quieter proposition!*

   *Look out for wild mountain goats along the next stretch of your walk - these feral creatures have survived in the Cheviot hills for 5,000*

On the approach to Windy Gyle

*years, and are shy and elusive – all the more reason to stop and rest awhile and scour the landscape, ideally with a pair of binoculars.*

Stay near to the fence (on your left) on this section of path, and this will lead you to a five-bar gate and stile. Cross the stile and follow the path steadily downhill to another gate and stile. The path now begins another steady climb (the last of the walk, you'll be pleased to hear) as it skirts around Swineside Law.

Keep walking with the fence on your left. Go over a stile beside a five-bar gate. At the corner where the fence turns off to the left at a gate you will also turn left following the fence line, ignoring the path which branches off here to your right.

6. The path skirts Hindside Knowe to another gate and continues with the fence on your left. When you reach a gate with a plethora of footpath signs, cross using the stile and continue straight ahead.

7. At a stile on the corner of the fence, turn sharp left. Now head steeply downhill to reach the car, which becomes visible on the roadside at the bottom of the hill.

*If you feel you need a stiff drink to celebrate the completion of such a wonderful walk, have an imaginary whisky with Black Rory. Your car is parked near the site of an 18th century inn at Slymefoot which served whisky produced at illicit distilleries in the valley. The most notorious whisky smuggler was Black Rory who used his knowledge of every hiding place in these hills and valleys to evade the patrolling Excisemen.*

# Walk 7
# Low Newton to Craster and Howick

*These two routes offer a seaside spectacular and a dramatic ruined castle. Instead of the Low Road walkers having an alternative route, they get a long rest in a lovely village while the High Roaders do an extension and return to the village. There are no steep hills, and underfoot is mainly short grass, sandy beach, or easy footpaths.*

| Distances | High Road 11.8 miles (18.9 kms) Low Road 7.7 miles (12.4 kms) |
|---|---|
| Duration | Approximately 6 hours |
| Parking | Pay and display car park on the only road into Low Newton (nearest sat nav postcode NE66 3EL). Car park is on the right, opposite the coastguard lookout cottage and just before the road descends to the village. Grid reference NU 239248 |
| Maps | Ordnance Survey Explorer 340 'Holy Island & Bamburgh' and Ordnance Survey Explorer 332 'Alnwick & Amble' |

## Walking Together

Leave the car park and turn right down the hill. Already you have a view of the sea and the beach, with Dunstanburgh Castle in the distance. At the bottom of the hill you walk onto the beach and head south, with the sea on your left.

*As you round the corner of the bay you'll see beach houses up on the dunes to your right – they were built in the 1930s and some have been in the same family for generations. They have no mains electricity and only have running water for part of the year. You will get a closer look at them later in the walk.*

53

Low Newton

1. A little further along you meet a stream crossing the beach. You can either wade this or turn right alongside it and follow the stream until you see the clubhouse for Dunstanburgh Castle Golf Club inland, which is open to non-members for refreshments. Ignore the first bridge on your left and take the second one, which has handrails, to return to the beach. Turn right and continue towards Dunstanburgh Castle.

   *Tucked into these dunes are several ugly concrete shelters. They are pillboxes, built during the Second World War as the final line of defence against an invasion. The first line of defence was the RAF, then the Royal Navy, but if they failed then troops in pillboxes around the country could hold off attackers long enough for mobile reinforcements to arrive. If they too failed, it was up to the Home Guard to do their bit. Don't panic Mr Mainwaring, don't panic...*

2. As you continue along the beach you will eventually run out of sand. At the rocks move right to join a path alongside the base of the dunes, gradually rising until you are on a cliff top path with the castle ahead luring you on through a gate.

   *You are now on the St Oswald's Way and Northumberland Coastal Path. In Spring and Summer you'll see thousands of kittiwakes nesting on the cliff face below the castle.*

   Follow the path beneath Dunstanburgh Castle, and keep curving left if you'd like to visit it (free to National Trust and English Heritage members). If not, then keep straight on between gorse bushes and down across a slightly marshy section towards the sea.

3. Head across a wide grassy area to a wooden gate, turn right and go through it to follow the track alongside the sea until you reach Craster.

4. Low Roaders will now have approximately 1½ hours to explore the village.

   *Craster used to be a busy fishing village, but these days you'll only see a few boats in the harbour. However, the famous Craster Kippers are still produced here by L Robson and Sons, a fourth-generation business that still cures the fish in the original smokehouses which are over 130 years old. The village also has a Tourist Information Centre, a café, an art gallery, and a pub.*

## High Road

4. As you come into Craster, follow the road round as it curves to the left. You will see the Jolly Fisherman on your left and Robson and Sons smokehouse on your right. When you reach the pub, take a left, following a public footpath sign – which indicates the Northumberland Coastal Path.

   Turn immediately right, and the path now takes you through the garden at the rear of the pub. Resisting the temptation to linger, continue along the narrow coastal path with the sea crashing on the rocks just below you to your left.

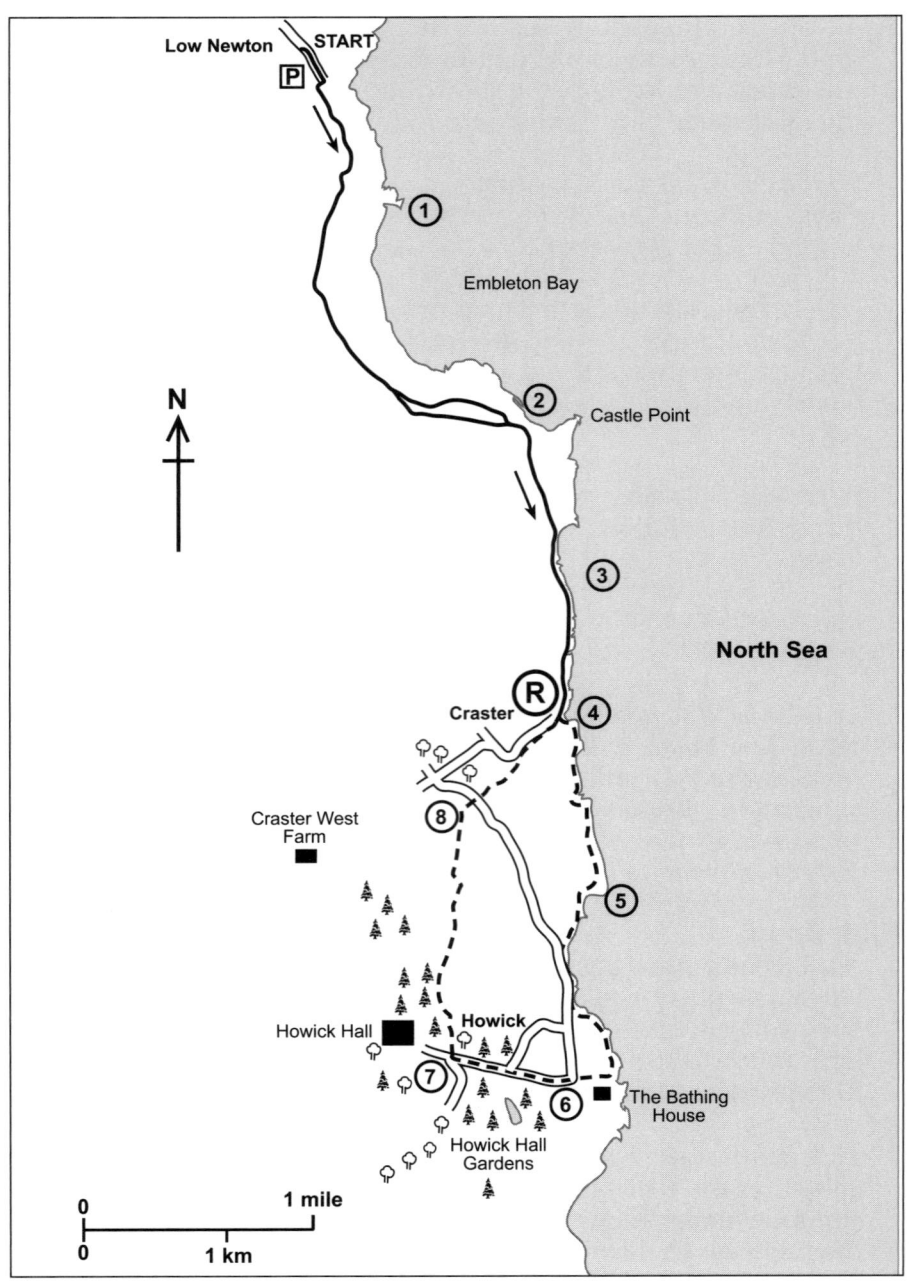

When you reach the edge of the village keep on straight ahead, still with the sea to your left. Pass through a kissing gate and the path takes you round an inlet. Soon you are on a broad grassy path that skirts the edge of the water.

*In sharp contrast to the golden sands of Low Newton where you started your walk, this part of the coastline is rocky and jagged. However, this is a delightful section of the walk, accompanied by the sight and sounds of the North Sea close by.*

Pass through another kissing gate and continue on the water's edge. After a few minutes walking, the path cuts in to the right heading slightly uphill. On the coastline ahead of you, you should see the distinctive chimneys of a dramatically sited house.

*This is the Bathing House, a popular holiday cottage and the most southerly point of your walk today.*

5. Pass through a kissing gate. A bench on your left allows for a lovely view of the nesting kittiwakes in the cliffs above the beach – a good place for a five-minute breather!

   Pass through another gate – the route now takes you close to the road with tall hedges on either side. Pass through another gate and after a few more minutes you will reach the Bathing House. Go past the cottage. Ahead of you is a lovely sandy beach. However, you are now going to leave the coast and head inland.

6. Turn sharp right, through the farm gate onto the broad track which leads to another gate onto a minor road. When you reach this second gate, go through it and onto the country lane ahead of you which will take for around ½ mile. Ignore the turning to Howick on your right, continuing straight on instead towards Howick Hall Gardens.

   *You are now walking along the edge of the gardens, which are renowned for their snowdrop displays in spring. The house on the estate owes its fame to being the home of Earl Grey tea – this was blended for Charles, the 2nd Earl Grey, in order to complement the taste of the water from the well at Howick.*

View of Dunstanburgh Castle

When you reach the entrance to Howick Hall and Gardens, turn right. There is a public footpath sign pointing towards Craster West Farm and Craster. You are now on a lovely broad track passing initially through woodland and then skirting open farmland. Whereas the early part of your walk was probably rather busy – especially if you've picked a weekend or school holidays – you may well have this next section all to yourself.

Ahead of you now is the dramatic escarpment of Howick Scar. At the edge of the field are two five-bar gates. Don't turn left but keep straight ahead, through the gate, and you will see a public footpath sign for Craster. You are now heading across the middle of a field on a clearly defined path.

Cross the wall at a ladder stile and bear slightly left, towards the edge of the escarpment, looking for a fingerpost and gate in the wall on the horizon straight ahead of you. Go through a kissing gate and follow the signs to Craster along the edge of another field. Ahead of you is Craster West Farm. When you reach it, follow the track round to the right to a minor road.

7. Turn left and then immediately right, following a footpath sign 'Craster ½ mile'. This is a lovely grassy path over the fields, heading for the trees which mark the outskirts of Craster village.

At the very bottom of the field, ignore one kissing gate on the left heading instead for one at the very furthest point of the field, which leads you into the old quarry at Craster Heugh. This is a whinstone outcrop and an important habitat for migrant and breeding birds. A lovely little stretch through here delivers you back into Craster village.

The path brings you to the car-park where there is a Tourist Information Centre and toilets. From here follow either the small footpath to your right or the road, back into the heart of the village. Here is where you will re-join your companions.

## Walking Together
Head back around the harbour and retrace your route to Dunstanburgh Castle. Although you have already walked this section

there's as much pleasure repeating it, with the springy grass underfoot, crashing sea to your right and this time, views of the castle ahead. Once you have passed the castle go through the gate.

*You might not have noticed on your outward walk a rocky promontory at sea level that's contorted and twisted into a wave formation. This is Greymare Rock, part of the Whin Sill geological formation that stretches across Northumberland. These rocks were once molten deep within the earth at temperatures as high as 1100 Celsius and they were squeezed up during a period of enormous earth movements.*

2. From the little gate head left around the golf green towards a blue waymaker on the fence. Follow the wide grassy track with a wire fence on your left and the golf course to your right.

   *Dunstanburgh Golf Club is a traditional links course, created by the Scottish golf course architect, James Braid in 1900. It started as nine holes and was gradually extended, with local fishermen doing the labour outside the fishing season. By 1932 they had 12 holes, and 15 by 1935. The golf course was maintained during this period by a six-foot wide horse-drawn cutter. Today the course has 18 holes.*

   Keep following the blue waymarkers and after a slight detour to cross an ornate footbridge on the golf course you reach a track where you will see the golf clubhouse up to your left. At the track you turn right following the signpost 'Coastpath and Low Newton by the Sea' then turn left alongside the stream and head straight on and up into the dunes to the fence on the skyline.

   Follow the path between the beach chalets. Ignore the footpath with yellow sign to the left and follow blue signs to Newton Pool Nature Reserve, which has a bird hide overlooking a big freshwater lagoon.

   The path reaches a wide sandy track beside a house – turn right along the track to reach a gate into the village. Go straight on between the cottages, then blue and yellow signs point to a right turn, which brings you out near to where you joined the beach. Go left, back up the road to your car.

# Walk 8
# Blaeberry Hill and the Carriage Drives

*Known as the Capital of Coquetdale, Rothbury makes a perfect start and end point for these walks. The routes follow clear paths and easy tracks through woods and heather moorland with great views of the surrounding hills. Once you have walked up the valley side from the village the gradients are gentle. There is little difference in the distances of the two routes, but the High Road follows a more arduous detour.*

| Distances | High Road 6.5 miles (10.5 kms)<br>Low Road 6.1 miles (9.8 kms) |
|---|---|
| Duration | Approximately 4 hours |
| Parking | Cowhaugh car park (pay and display) Whitton Bank Road on the south bank of the River Coquet in Rothbury (nearest sat nav postcode NE65 7RX). Grid reference NU 057015. Public toilets near the footbridge |
| Map | Ordnance Survey Explorer 332 'Alnwick & Amble' |

## Walking Together

Leave the car park over the bridge and walk up into the village. Turn right along the main street until you reach the Queen's Head pub.

1. Turn left onto Brewery Lane, following the road steadily round to the right up the hill.

    *You will pass Addycombe Cottages, originally built for workers on the Cragside Estate of Lord Armstrong, the Victorian inventor and engineer.*

    Follow the main road past the cottages, and the modern bungalows of Addycombe Gardens. Rothbury First School is on your left. Take the first turning to your left and head for a gate into a field – go

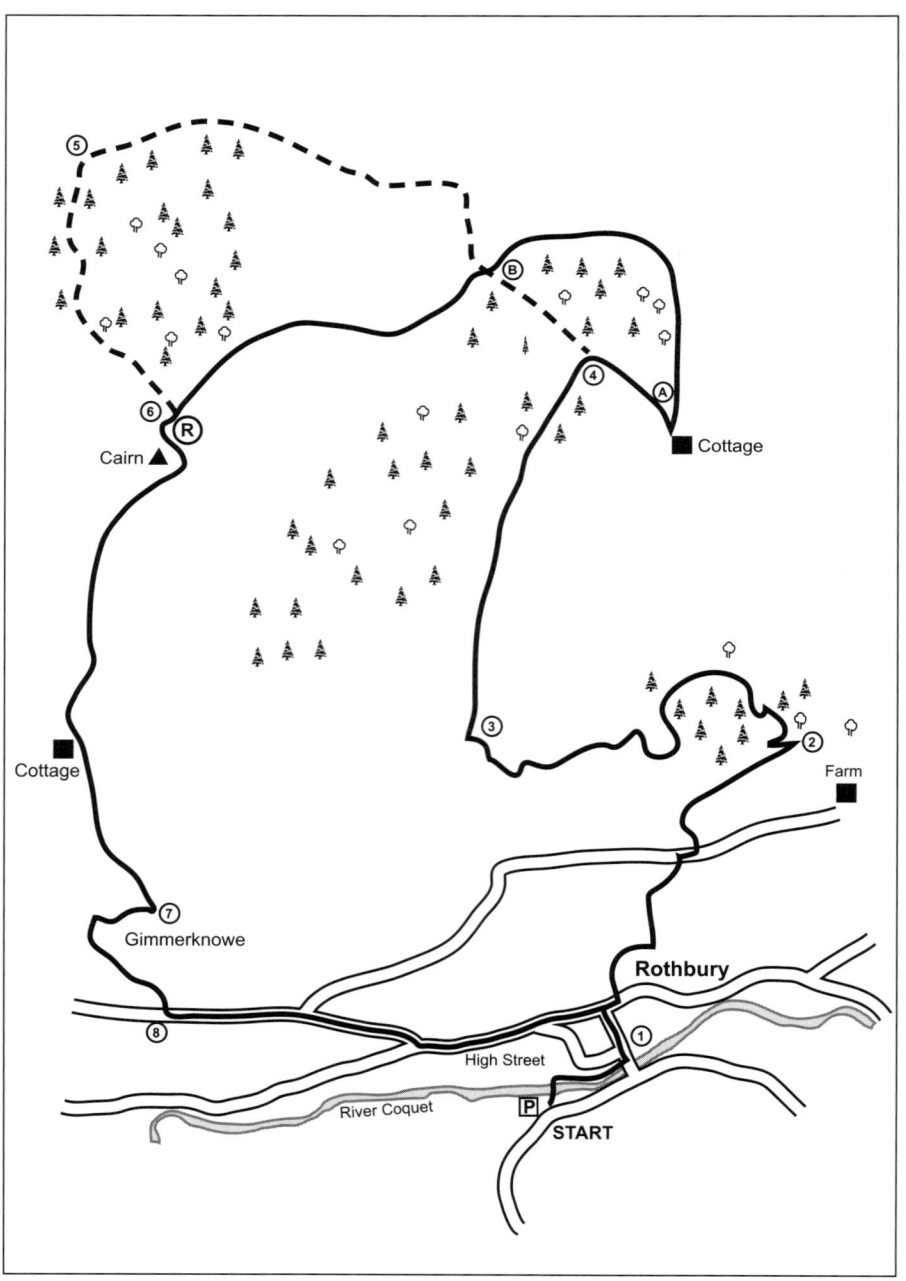

through this following a public footpath 'Alnwick Road ¾ mile'. This path winds up the hill. At the road and a row of houses, turn right and keep straight ahead as the road becomes more of a track. After a couple of minutes you will reach a footpath sign and wooden steps over a wall. Cross the wall into a field. Follow the path diagonally right and up across this field towards woodland ahead. Halfway up the field, go through a gate, and continue upwards with a wire fence on your right. You may well see amenable Highland cattle and other rare breeds here.

2. At the top of the field, go through a kissing gate and turn left.

   *You are now on the Carriage Drives, created by Lord Armstrong for scenic carriage rides around his property. Most of the Cragside Estate now belongs to the National Trust, however the land you are walking on today still belongs to the Armstrong Estate. Before you head into the woodland, take time to admire the distant views of Simonside. The village of Rothbury is now spread out below you.*

   Where the path forks, keep to the right hand, upper path, as it winds through beech woods, ignoring any temptations to veer off down the hill.

   *After around ½ mile look out for a bird feeding area – if you are lucky you might spot red squirrels here too.*

3. Another ½ a mile or so brings you to a gate leading out onto open moorland. Go through the kissing gate and then take the path immediately to your right (indicated by a fingerpost) which crosses the open moorland of Blaeberry Hill.

   *Blaeberries have a number of other names such as bilberry, whortleberry and whinberry. They grow well on these hills, ripening to a dark blue colour in July and August.*

   As you cross the moorland a little footbridge takes you over a peat burn.

   *Shortly before you reach the woodland at the end of the moor, look out for a little stone which marks the county boundary between*

Rothbury (R) and Debdon (D). From this point you can see the estate cottages of the Cragside Estate to the east.

When you reach the edge of the moorland, cross another burn and head for a gate. Go through it and turn right onto a broad forestry track, following a waymarker.

4. After ¼ mile you reach a T-junction. This is where you split into two groups.

## High Road

Go left, signposted 'Snitter', and walk up the forest road to reach a crossroads of tracks. Go straight on, heading north (if in doubt, that is the middle of the three gateways – it does not have a waymarker, although it is a public right of way).

Boundary stone on the moors outside Rothbury

Go through the gate and head uphill on a red gravel track. Keep straight ahead, ignoring a waymarker on your left. As the road curves around to the left, there are glorious views of the Cheviots.

Go through another gate and continue straight ahead. Ahead of you are the remains of Cartington Castle.

*The actual date of the castle is uncertain, although it is mentioned in 1416 in the list of Border fortresses and in 1421 it was extended. In 1648 the castle was besieged and taken by parliamentary forces. A few years later it was dismantled and the stones used to build barns and walls. Lord Armstrong did some restoration work in 1887, to prevent the castle from collapsing. It stands on private land.*

5. As you round the corner, you will see a Forest Enterprise sign for Blue Mill woodland. Turn left here and head steadily uphill.

   At the edge of the woods, the path narrows. Keep straight ahead following a waymarker.

   Just as the trees finish as you come round the hill, look out for a footpath waymarker on your right – turn right and follow the narrow path uphill.

   Cross the stone wall by way of a stone stepping-stile and the path now climbs up through the heather, re-joining the main track at the top of the hill.

6. The rendezvous point is a cairn with multiple yellow waymarker arrows opposite a conifer plantation.

## Low Road

4. At the split point turn right, signposted 'Alnwick Road', and continue along the forestry track until you reach a five bar gate. There is a cottage on your right.

A. Then turn left through another gate, signposted 'Thropton and Rothbury'.

   You can afford time to dawdle along this lovely section of grassy path, with open moorland on your right and Primrose Woods on your left. Go through another gate and continue on the broad grassy track.

B. At the next gate you get to a crossroads of tracks – go straight on, signposted 'Thropton and Rothbury'.

   Stay on the forest track as it curves to the right and climbs. The Simonside Ridge gradually comes into view on your left. As you proceed, the scenery continues to open out and you gain panoramic views of the Cheviot Hills to your right.

   After you pass a wood on your right look out for a cairn with a four-way marker on your right. This is the rendezvous point.

## Walking Together

6. Continue ahead on the broad track. As you come round the hill, look out on your right-hand side for a grassy path which leads through the heather towards a gap in the drystone wall.

   Don't go through the gap in the wall but instead turn left and walk with the wall on your right. Where the wall bears right, continue straight ahead on the wide grassy track. The track becomes a cement road at Whinhams Cottage. Carry on along this track with a lake down below you on the right.

7. Halfway up the next hill turn right following the sign for Gimmerknowe, and just before the cottage go left and alongside a stone wall.

   *Views of the River Coquet appear. The land in the valley bottom was a steeplechase course for more than two hundred years. The last*

View of Cartington Castle

*race was in 1965, and the area now hosts the much more sedate sport of golf.*

Cross a ladder stile into a wood. A narrow path takes you down to pass between two houses and reach the tarmac lane.

8. Turn left and keep on this lane gradually downhill until you get to Rothbury, when you go left along the high street, offering a choice of pubs, cafés and other delights. You'll see to your right the return path to the car park, beside the vet's surgery and roughly opposite the Turk's Head pub.

# Walk 9
# Simonside Ridge and Spylaw

*These routes give terrific views for relatively little effort. The longer route loops south of the Simonside ridge with some rough and wet terrain. Dogs must be kept on the lead across Access Land. The easier walk goes north of the ridge mainly on forest tracks. Both routes meet to return along the crest of Simonside. There's a short steep scramble to the top of Simonside, and some stepped descents.*

| Distances | High Road 6.5 miles (10km)<br>Low Road 4.5 miles (7.2 km), or 4.7 miles (7.6 km) with the detour to Church Rock |
|---|---|
| Duration | Approximately 4½ hours |
| Parking | The Northumberland National Park car park at Lordenshaws on the B6342, south of Rothbury (nearest sat nav postcode NE61 4PU). Grid reference NZ 053 988 |
| Map | Ordnance Survey Explorer Map OL42 'Kielder Water and Forest' |

## Walking Together
Cross the road and go up the path opposite the car park, signposted Spylaw and Coquet Cairn.

*The climb is helped by solid stone steps put in to control erosion of the sandy soil. You will have more reason later to be grateful for the herculean efforts of the National Park Voluntary Rangers and others who manoeuvred the stones into place.*

1. On this walk the split point comes quite early and your party separates at the first waymarker, about five minutes up the hill. In

a role reversal of most walks in this book, the Low Roaders now go uphill while the High Roaders head across the moor then downhill.

## High Road

At the split point go left (marked St Oswald's Way). The path heads through heather to a bridge made of railway sleepers across the Grain Sike burn. After crossing this, follow the clear track around and up the hill to a gate in the fence ahead of you.

When you reach the gate, turn right (don't go through the gate). Keeping the fence on your left, walk to another gate, which crosses the track in front of you. Cross the ladder stile. On your right is a new plantation, and in front of it, a large stone painted with the word Spylaw. This is the name of the old farmhouse towards which you are heading.

Follow the track straight ahead. Where two gates cross the path, take the one on the left and head for the wood, surrounded by a stone wall. Turn left in front of the wall and head through the long grass until you reach Spylaw house.

*The old farmhouse was abandoned for many years – not surprisingly, given its remote location. It now has a new purpose in life as a camping barn, used by groups as a base for outdoor activities. The views to the south from the front of the house are typical of the open vistas and big skies which you get in this corner of England.*

2. Cross the stile in front of Spylaw house and turn right, heading in front of a plantation. Beyond the plantation, cross another stile over a fence. Carry on downhill and cross a small burn. Now follow the waymarkers which take you across rough ground with duckboards in places to the Forest Burn (signposted Public Footpath). Cross using the wooden bridge, and head uphill on the track.

When you reach a junction of paths at the top of the hill, go straight ahead following waymarkers over the moorland to a fence on the horizon. Cross using the stile, and then turn right, following the path over the hill towards the edge of the forest. Here you will find the Coquet Cairn.

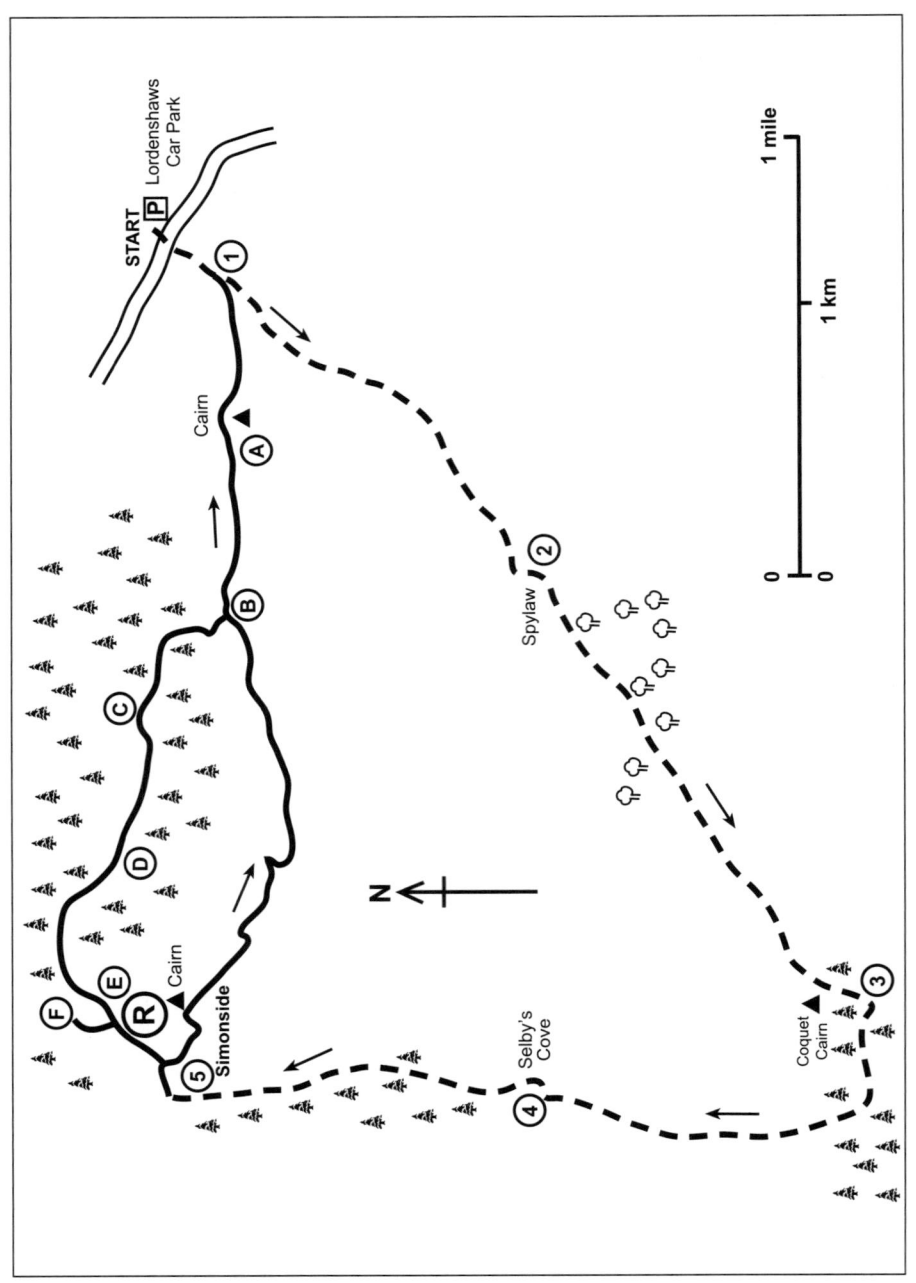

*This Cairn is sited at 982 feet. It marks the high point of the long-distance St Oswald's Way footpath – you, however, will shortly be climbing up to 1,410 feet on the Simonside Ridge.*

3. From the Cairn, use the stile close to the corner to cross the fence and follow the path leading into the forest. This soon becomes a broad track. Turn right and carry on to the forest road. Turn right on this road and then, almost immediately (where the road bends), turn right again, heading along a grassy track to the edge of the forest. Cross the fence using the stile next to the gate and, using the waymarkers, head towards Selby's Cove. This area is wet in places but duck-boards will take you across the worst of the boggy ground.

*The sandstone cove was reputed to be the hideout of the renowned Border Reiver Black Walter. Border Reivers were cattle-rustlers and smugglers who plagued this area between the 13th and 17th centuries.*

4. Continuing to follow the waymarkers, head uphill towards the edge of the trees on your left. Cross the fence into the forest and walk down through the trees. Cross three small bridges and continue. Extensive felling here in recent years means that the forest is changing all the time, but the path is way-marked. It brings you, uphill, onto a track along the edge of the forest where it meets with a road. Turn left here and walk for a couple of minutes until you reach the rendezvous point. This is clearly identified by three benches, at a viewpoint below the craggy outline of Simonside.

## Low Road

At the split point you go right and head gradually uphill. The path is eroded and rocky in places, but not too rugged or steep, and already you are getting stunning views. That's the reward for temporarily being a High Roader!

*On the far horizon to the left you'll see a giant golf ball – an RAF surveillance radar on Alnwick Moor. A little down and to the right of the golf ball Cragside is the huge house surrounded by trees. The Cragside Estate is a National Trust property.*

*The single cylindrical tower you can see south of Rothbury is Sharp's Folly, built by Thomas Sharp the rector of Rothbury in the mid eighteenth century. Its plaque reads "Erected for the relief of unemployment amongst local stonemasons" and Rev Sharp used it as an observatory to study the stars.*

A. Ten minutes after splitting from your companions you reach a big untidy stone cairn and have views of the Cheviot Hills ahead of you. Continue on the path from the cairn down an inviting white sandy track. Within the view to your left the glinting water is Fontburn Reservoir.

B. Half way down the slope you turn off to the right, but the start of this path through the heather is indistinct. You will see the end of the path in the distance at roughly 45 degrees to the main path, pointing towards the Cheviot Hills and the left end of a plantation in the foreground. Where this path leaves the main track is just faintly marked in the heather but a short distance on and you will be on a much clearer path which takes you to a wire fence.

C. Cross the rather rickety stile and go straight on. If you miss the path through the heather, or don't fancy a rickety stile, you just stay on the main track and go through the small wooden gate ahead of you. Then immediately go right, with a wire fence to your right. This path can be a bit squelchy. When you reach the rickety stile on your right the path turns left and you are walking parallel to the ridge.

Soon the path widens out into a sandy track which goes straight on and gradually downhill passing a Forestry Commission red waymarker.

D. This white sandy track reaches a T-junction with a red gravel forest track – turn left, uphill. This is a very steady ascent with the forest on your right and the ridge to your left. You pass a little pond surrounded by a wooden fence on your right, and you might see rock climbers inching up the crags on your left.

Just a little further up the track you reach three benches, each at a different angle to make the most of the wide views of Coquetdale

Simonside

and the Cheviot Hills. An information panel identifies the summits on the horizon.

E. The benches are the rendezvous point but you should have time for an interesting little detour: walk a little uphill from the benches, turn right at a marker post without any arrows on it and head down through the heather to enter the forest. This path is quite steep and very eroded, with tricky gullies between rocks so assess your energy levels before making the detour!

F. Your objective is 'Little Church Rock', a massive stone outcrop on the right of the path.

*This is thought to have been the location for illicit preaching in medieval times. A few yards further down there's another oddity – the path goes across a long rock which has been carved with grooves and squares. Their origin is a mystery, with theories ranging from prehistoric decorations to an attempt to create a non-slip surface for pack horses or the ponies of whisky smugglers.*

You might feel the need of a slug of whisky to get you back up the rocky path to the rendezvous point at the three benches.

## Walking Together
With the three benches behind you turn right uphill along the track. Soon the main track curves to the right and you go left in the direction of a marker with a white arrow on a red background.

5. An information panel stands near the bottom of a steep upwards path which you take to get you to the top of Simonside. There are plenty of good handholds at the steepest sections and in just a few minutes you will be gazing at one of the best 360-degree views in Northumberland – just go left for a few yards and you reach the cairn at the summit at 1,410 feet.

   There follows a ridge walk that lifts the spirits through a combination of wide views, moorland scenery and easy walking on solid flagstones.

*The flagstones were brought in to protect the sandstone and peat, the vegetation and archaeological sites from erosion. The stones had a previous life as floors in old mills. The Northumberland National Park Authority lifted 450 tonnes of stone onto the ridge by helicopter, then manhandled flagstones on the level sections of the path, and large blocks on the steep slopes to create steps.*

Route-finding for the remainder of the walk is easy – just follow the path along the ridge. It dips and deviates a little, passing huge boulders leaning against each other to form nooks and crannies. Eventually you reach a wooden gate across the path. go through this and follow the inviting sandy track up to Beacon Crag. You'll see the car park below you.

# Walk 10
# Bolam Lake and Shaftoe Crags

*Northumberland has a huge variety of landscapes and this walk explores its pastoral and arable side. Paths are mostly across or alongside fields, although the route cuts through the dramatic rocks of Shaftoe Crags. Bolam Lake Country Park adds woodland and waterside to the delights you will experience. The few ascents are short and gradual.*

| Distances | High Road 8.9 miles (14.3 kms)<br>Low Road 7.6 miles (12.2 kms) |
|---|---|
| Duration | Approximately 5 hours |
| Parking | Boathouse Wood Car Park at Bolam Lake Country Park (nearest sat nav postcode NE20 0HE). Pay and display parking (car park locked at dusk), café, information centre, toilets. Grid reference NZ 084820 |
| Map | Ordnance Survey Explorer Map OL42 'Kielder Water and Forest' |

## Walking Together
Leave the car park and walk down to the water, turning left along the lakeside path.

*You pass a large metal standpipe. When it functioned as a water pump horses and carts would line up to collect water from it.*

Continue past the Low House Wood car park, still on the lakeside. When you reach the West Wood car park, walk straight across it and out the other side. You will exit along a path next to a blue sign reminding motorists to pay and display and continue in a line parallel with the road.

1. When you come to a junction of tracks beside an entrance from the road, take the path to the left, marked by a small stump with 'no horses' and 'no cyclists' signs on it. The path starts as gravel underfoot and runs alongside the road, weaving though the trees. Continue along until you come to the corner of the country park and you'll see a road sign saying 'Harnham'.

2. Leave the country park here and turn right along the quiet tarmac road.

3. At the cross roads beside a postbox, turn left onto a bridleway signposted 'Shaftoemoor'. You reach a gate and cattle grid and the track becomes a broad grassy path. Go straight ahead, with a wall on your right. Continue up the grassy track until you reach the top of the hill. Go through the gate and continue straight ahead.

4. When you reach the crest of the hill the path descends into a gully – this is Salter's Nick, part of an old drove road which cuts through dramatic sandstone crags.

   *You might wish to visit the trig point on the top of Shaftoe Crags at this point. If so, from the bottom of Salter's Nick take the path that leads off left and you can head uphill just after Shaftoe Grange. There are plenty of nice rocks to rest on at Salter's Nick for those who don't wish to add this onto their walk!*

   Once you've re-grouped at Salter's Nick, continue downhill towards the aptly-named Half Moon Plantation. Go through a five bar gate and continue to follow the bridleway straight ahead.

5. After a couple more metal gates you reach a junction of stone walls. Look out for a stone stepping stile built into the wall on your right, use this to cross the wall and then turn half-right diagonally across the middle of the field towards a roof-top which is just visible at this point. This is easy going apart from one muddy section in the middle. You are aiming for a gate in the wall which is to the right of the roof-top. Go through the gate and head straight on towards a stone wall corner.

6. Go right at the corner and walk along with the wall on your right until you reach the corner of the field, where a way-marker points you left.

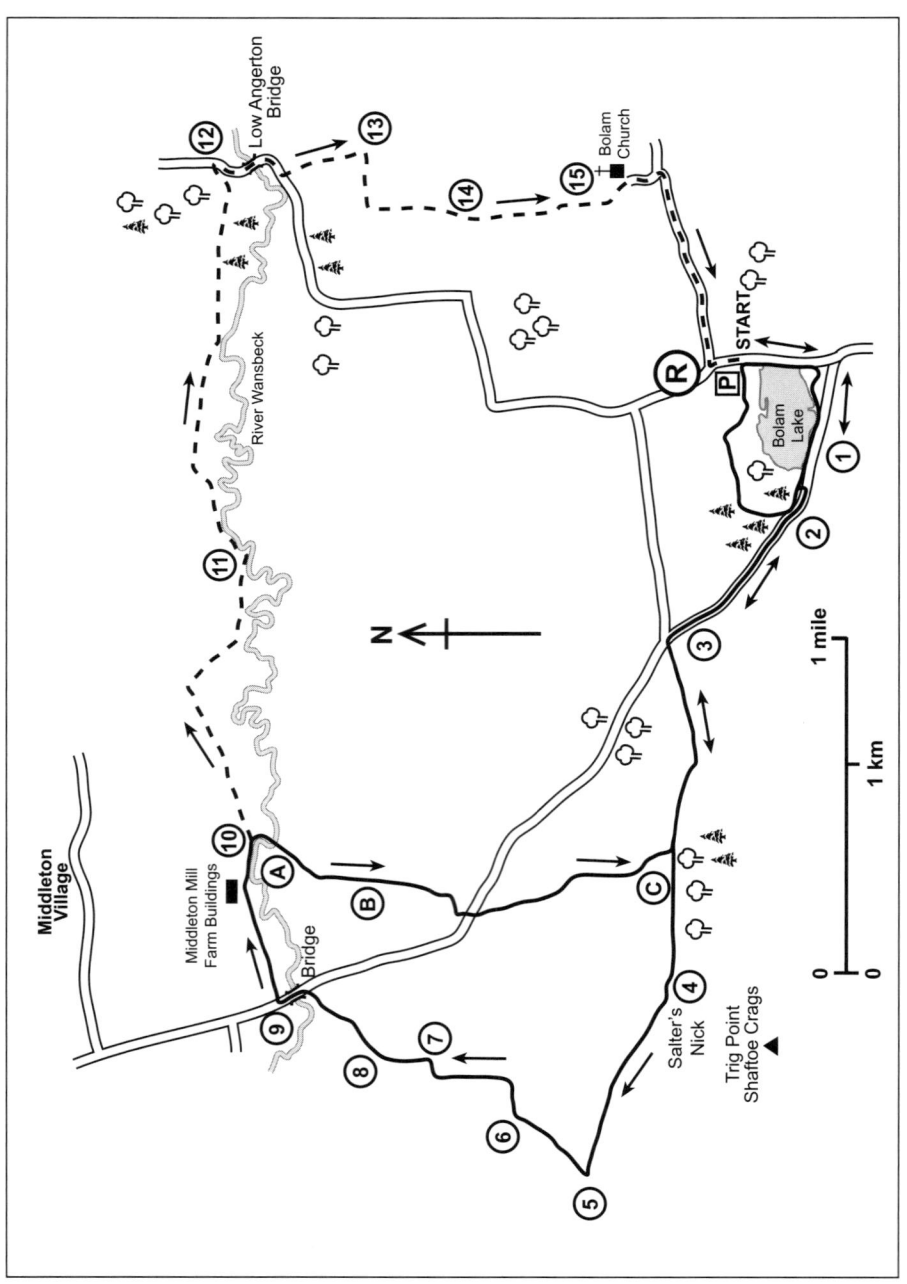

7. Walking with another wall on your right, you head directly towards Middleton South Farm. Go through the gate and walk in front of the house. Just before a set of gateposts, look for the last in a series of gates which has a way-marker on it.

8. Go left through this gate and walk on, keeping a stone wall and line of beech trees on your left. Just beyond the trees, look for a gate on your left. Go through this and turn right, with the wall now on your right. Halfway alongside a wood, you will see a large stone crescent-shaped wall. This is where you veer left, downhill, passing to the right of the wall.

   Head towards the far right and corner of the field (you might be able to see a footpath sign in the distance). Cross a small stream via a footbridge then head slightly left up the bank to reach the road.

   *On either side of the road are the remains of South Middleton Village, first recorded in 1296 and deserted by the mid-18th century. The outlines of field systems and rectangular houses are most visible when a low sun casts shadows of the mounds and ridges.*

9. Turn left onto the road, cross the road bridge, and turn immediately right onto a bridleway, signposted 'Middleton Mill'.

   When you enter the farm, look out for footpath signs which will direct you to the right towards the river, and then left around the farm buildings with the River Wansbeck now on your right.

   Exit the farm via a metal gate and then a wooden gate, and carry on towards the footbridge still with the river on your right to reach another wooden gate.

10. After the gate you walk around to your right to a footbridge which is where the group splits.

## High Road

10. With your back to the footbridge and with the River Wansbeck on your right, continue across the field towards a steel gate. Go through and continue, veering slightly left, towards another gate

which has a sign beside it warning of overhead electric power lines. Go through the gate then walk diagonally left, away from the river, following a line of telegraph poles across the field.

Almost at the edge of the field cross a wide planked bridge in front of a wooden gate, but do not go through the gate. Instead, turn right, and follow the line of the fence on your left, heading back towards the river. Carry on along a broad green grassy track towards a fence and some farm buildings on the horizon ahead. Go through a metal gate and you are now back beside the River Wansbeck. Continue in the same direction, heading for a large clump of trees. Ignore another gate in the fence and do not turn off before the wood.

11. When you reach the trees, pass through a gate and turn immediately left, heading around the wood (which will be on your right) on a broad grassy track.

Go through another gate at the back of the woods and, ignoring the footpath sign, continue straight ahead on the bridleway. The river is still on your right, although you will start to head away from it, and you are now aiming for a gate in the fence by a line of hawthorn trees.

Go through the gate and straight across the dismantled railway line.

*This is the former Wansbeck Railway, known locally as the "Wannie Line". It ran from Morpeth to Redesmouth, opened in 1865 and closed in 1966.*

Exit the railway line via another gate and continue straight ahead on the raised broad grass track, again cutting the corner of the field. At the end of this field, go through another small wooden gate and follow on to another gate. Head towards the woods. Beside the woods is another gate. Go through this and continue on with the woods on your right.

12. When you reach the end of that field, you exit via a small wooden gate onto a tarmac country lane. Turn right. The road takes you

over the River Wansbeck and round to the right past Low Angerton. Just beyond the farm buildings, turn left through a gate at a public footpath sign to Bolam. Go straight on to cross a stile and continue uphill at the edge of the field.

13. At the far corner of this field, turn to the right, with a fence on your left. Towards the end of the fence, turn left (way-marked) and cross the corner of the field to reach a kissing gate. You now cross the old railway line again to pass through another wooden gate into a field.

    Walk uphill to reach a big metal gate on your right with a public footpath sign. Go through the gate and continue in the same direction but with the fence now on your left.

14. Walk past Angerton Steads. Go through the gate beside the tennis court and bungalow, then turn left through a metal gate. Head uphill with the fence now back on your right.

    When you reach the end of this field do not go over the stile in the right-hand corner, but turn left and walk along a few metres down into a second corner and through a gate with a yellow waymarker.

15. The path weaves between tussocky mounds towards a telegraph pole. You are aiming for a five-bar gate to the right of the church which you can now see nestled in the trees up ahead. Go through the gate at the top of the field, follow the path left and then upwards to pass thorough two gates into the churchyard.

*It is worth taking a few minutes to explore St Andrew's Church which dates back to Saxon times, and even survived being hit by a bomb in World War II. The small window on the south wall is where the bomb landed and crashed into the church without exploding. The churchyard has many unusual headstones, some decorated with skull and crossbones carvings.*

Exit the churchyard and go straight on along the driveway. At the road, turn right and walk along to pass the impressive Bolam Hall.

*This Grade II listed building dates back to 1810. It was built by Robert Horsley for his daughter Charlotte Philadelphia on her*

Bolam Church

*marriage to John Beresford, the Baron Decies. Bolam Hall is now divided into two units – West Wing and East Wing.*

At the end of the road is a T-Junction. You will see the road sign to Bolam Lake Country Park, but you do not need to walk along the road. Simply cross to the stile and follow the path through the woods to reach a wide track, where you turn left and walk back to your car beside the café and visitor centre, which you will come to almost immediately.

## Low Road

10. Your companions stay to the north of the River Wansbeck, but you cross the footbridge, turn left and then head up the field diagonally to your right. Pass the remains of a stone wall and continue across to reach a wooden gate under a big sycamore tree.

A. Now go straight up across the next field, heading for a red metal gate next to a stone wall. Through that gate you follow an obvious grassy track for a short distance, then veer slightly right to pass a fence corner which juts out to your right.

B. Head for the buildings of Bank Top Farm and go into the farmyard through another gate. Turn left through the yard and you reach the road. Cross over and take the track signposted 'Public Footpath East Shaftoe Hall'. This starts as a tarmac track then becomes a lovely grassy path crossing pastureland studded with rock slabs. Where the track is less distinct, just aim for the single wind turbine ahead and eventually you'll come to a small gate in the wall, located to the right of a patch of trees and rhododendrons.

C. Pass through this and turn left, and you have rejoined your outward route. Retrace your steps by going over the cattle grid, back along the lane, and turn right onto the road. Further down the road you'll recognise the entrance to Bolam Lake Country Park on your left, next to the signpost for Harnham. Go into the park and turn right, along the woodland path.

D. At West Wood Car Park, instead of continuing to retrace your outward path, turn left half way along the car park and follow the wooden boardwalk. At the end of this just make your way around the lake, with the water on your right, along obvious paths until you come to the visitor centre and café. This is the rendezvous point.

# Walk 11
# Elsdon and Landshot Hill

*From a peaceful village that has a violent past you walk a circuit around a formerly lawless landscape. Both routes cross pasture and use farm and forest roads to gain wide views with relatively little effort.*

| Distances | High Road 6 miles (9.7km)<br>Low Road 4 miles (6.4km) |
|---|---|
| Duration | Approximately 2¾ hours |
| Parking | The small car park at the north end of the village, beside the bridge over the Elsdon Burn (nearest sat nav postcode NE19 1AB). Grid reference NY 937932 |
| Map | Ordnance Survey Explorer OL 42 'Kielder Water & Forest' |

## Walking Together
Leave via the rear of the car park and walk to the left of the village hall following the Public Bridleway sign up a narrow lane.

*The lumps and bumps of land on your left are the remains of a 12th century motte and bailey castle – there's an information panel about the defences as you reach a house further up.*

At the house go straight on and through a wooden gate into a field, still following the public bridleway sign. Head uphill with a wire fence and trees on your left.

1. Go through the gate and walk diagonally right across a big field heading for a gate and line of trees.

2. Through that gate you walk alongside a line of wizened hawthorn trees to reach a gate onto a tarmac lane. By now you have increasingly wide views of the hills surrounding Elsdon.

Turn left across the cattle grid and down the lane, over another cattle grid, and downhill to a row of cottages at Hudspeth.

3. At the end of the terrace go through a gate and immediately right. After a gate bear left climbing a grassy bank to a vague path. As you climb you will see a gate in a post-and-wire fence. Aim for this and once through it take a left diagonal route upwards as views of the Cheviot Hills appear.

4. The path is unclear, but eventually you will see a metal gate with a stile, next to a wall corner. Here the routes split.

## High Road

4. Go over the stile and walk gently uphill next to the wall on your right until you reach a ladder stile. Go over the stile and turn left, slightly downhill diagonally on a nice grassy track – there are occasional way-markers and you are heading for another stone wall. At the wall there is a stepping stile built into the stonework.

   *These clever stiles almost seem to disappear into the drystone walls – they are far less obtrusive and more fun than a wooden one – you are about to encounter a series of these.*

5. Keep following the path in the same direction using way-markers and keeping the edge of the conifer plantation on your left-hand side.

   *This section of path can be overgrown in places. The patch of heather moorland is*

Stone stepping stile

85

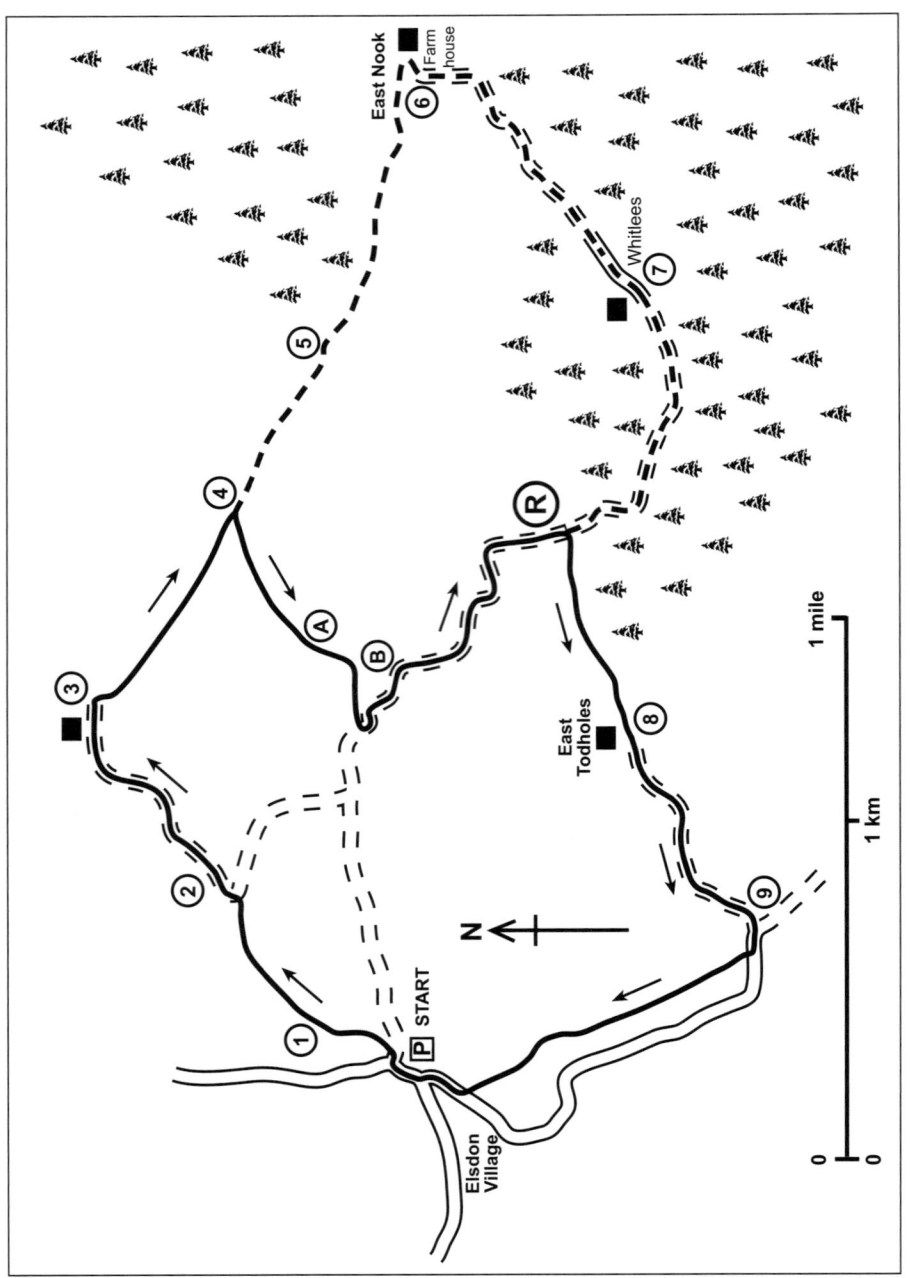

*Access Land and is particularly stunning in the summer when the heather is in bloom.*

Soon you reach another wall and, yes, another stone stepping stile to cross by. Walk now with the wall on your left towards East Nook farmhouse which you can see ahead of you in the trees. Prepare for muddy sections, with the promise of a nice dry tarmac road soon. When you reach the wall separating you from the farmhouse, there is another stone stile to cross.

6. Keep heading for the farmhouse until you reach the road, and then turn right at a cattle grid, heading away from the farm.

*The metal signs with triangles indicate where the sides of the road are after snowfall.*

Continue along the road, through a metal gate, and uphill towards Whitlees. Once through the gate, you walk through a conifer plantation, and as the trees start to thin out you'll see Whitlees ahead of you.

*At the bottom of the garden to your right is a former bastle – there are many of these fortified farmhouses in Northumberland, built in the late 16th and early 17th centuries to protect local people against raiders from both sides of the Scottish Border.*

7. Carry on straight ahead on the tarmac road. You will wind steadily downhill through trees to reach a wooden five-bar gate – this is your rendezvous point with the rest of the group. Note the signpost on the left hand side before you reach the gate as this will be the next part of the walk.

## Low Road
4. At the metal gate and wall-corner do not cross the stile, but turn right and descend with the wall on your left. Further down you'll see a stone wall ahead, at right angles to your direction, with a gateway flanked by two big stone gateposts.

A. There isn't an obvious path, but go through the gateway and straight ahead until you reach a small waymaker post with a yellow sign pointing right to a small bridge. Cross this, and go uphill to the ladder stile on the left of the farm buildings at Landshot.

B. On the other side of the stile turn left along the tarmac lane downhill. Cross the bridge with white railings, continue on and ignore the footbridge on your right signposted East Todholes.

*The metal posts with triangular flags mark the road edge in winter when the snow is deep.*

Stay on the tarmac lane across a cattle grid and another bridge with white railings, passing the driveway to Whiskershiel Farm. Ahead is a wooden gate at the entrance to the forest, and that is your rendezvous point.

## Walking Together

From the wooden gate, retrace the High Road steps a few yards and turn right onto a bridleway leading through the trees. Cross the little footbridge over the burn. You are now in the Mill Burn Nature Reserve, which is managed by the Northumberland Wildlife Trust.

*It's an unusual narrow strip of grassland within the forest and is home to the rare plants green spleenwort fern, grass-of-Parnassus and blue moor grass.*

A lovely little path now leads through the woods, although it can be a bit boggy. Go over another little footbridge, all well-waymarked, and continue along the bridleway.

8. As you leave the woods, go through a gate and onto the road at East Todholes, a farmstead that dates back to the 16th Century. Tod means fox – it is an Anglo-Saxon word.

    *When you reach the top of the hill, past the farm, you get a fabulous view – behind you is the whole of your circuit so far, including the High Roaders' hill. Nestled in the bowl below you is Elsdon village, with the Mote Hills, where you started, clearly visible to the right.*

9. At the end of the lane, you reach a T-Junction onto a main road. Turn right, and then, immediately, right again, crossing a stile at a

footpath sign 'Elsdon ½ mile'. Cut across the field bearing half left and downhill, towards a stile in the fence ahead.

Cross the stile and, with another fence on your left, carry on downhill aiming for the bridge ahead of you. Cross the fence using a stile, and then cross the large wooden bridge over the burn. Bear left on a clearly defined path, heading for the houses on the outskirts of Elsdon village.

Cross another, much smaller, wooden bridge. You should now be able to see the footbridge on your left where you will re-enter the village. To reach it you might need to skirt around an area of marshy ground.

Once through the gate, walk between the houses and straight ahead, into the centre of the village.

*There used to be a cock-fighting pit on the green, and a bear baiting site is marked by a stone near the bus stop. The circular enclosure is the 18th century pinfold where stray livestock were kept.*

The village has a pub and a café. To return to the car park simply turn right, passing a row of historic cottages.

*One is Bacchus House with a statue of the god on his wine barrel above the front door – this used to be an inn, as were Crown Farm and Raylees Farm.*

## Walk 12
# Kielder Water: Leaplish to Tower Knowe

*On these routes you can stride along smooth paths enjoying changing views of Kielder Reservoir and the surrounding countryside. Artworks and viewpoints add interest along the route, and the Lakeside Way is suitable for mobility scooters and wheelchair users. This is a linear walk – either park at Tower Knowe Visitor Centre and get the Osprey Ferry to Leaplish Waterside Park, or use two cars leaving one at Tower Knowe and taking the other to the start point at Leaplish.*

| Distances | High Road 7.5 miles (12 km)<br>Low Road 4.5 miles (7 km) |
|---|---|
| Duration | Approximately 3½ hours |
| Parking | If you are in a group with two cars, you can leave one at Tower Knowe Visitor Centre (grid reference NY 698868) and all go in the second to Leaplish Waterside Park (grid reference NY 660877). A nicer option is to park your car at Tower Knowe (nearest sat nav postcode NE48 1BX) and get the ferry to Leaplish. The Osprey motor cruiser runs from the end of March to the end of October (check details at Leaplish 01434 251000, Tower Knowe 01434 240436 or www.visitkielder.com). Both car parks are pay and display, and have information centres, cafés and toilets |
| Map | Ordnance Survey Explorer OL 42 'Kielder Water & Forest' |

## Walking Together
Exit the Leaplish car park following the Lakeside Way. To find the path, with the lake behind you, head towards the swimming pool building and you will see a pedestrian crossing with a big sign which says "Cycles and Horses". Follow that, turning left onto the Lakeside

Way. The path heads gently uphill – where it forks, take the middle option through the trees.

*After a few minutes you reach a woodland hide. If you are lucky, this is an excellent place to spot red squirrels. Also keep your eyes peeled for art works – the area has an award-winning collection of visual art and architecture. Near to you is 'Shadow' snaking down the grassy bank towards the water. It's made from local whinstone, sandstone and earth and is designed to echo the many textures on the ancient beech trees.*

1. After about 1¼ miles of walking on an excellent path, you come to a three-way fingerpost. This is where the group splits, but it is well worth everyone pausing to visit Freya's Cabin, a unique wooden fairy-tale hut with a story to tell.

## High Road

1. Drop down to the wide track below Freya's Cabin, turn right and walk alongside the water. You might expect a lakeside path to be flat – however, this one is surprisingly undulating.

   *As you walk, you can enjoy the beautiful views out across the lake (and if you pause to look behind you, into the hills of southern Scotland).*

   After about a mile of walking the path becomes a tarmac road for a short while – mainly for the use of forestry vehicles – but then after half a mile or so you are back on the lovely forest path.

2. This now heads right, slightly away from the water and into the woods. Around half an hour after separating from the other group, you will

Kielder Water view

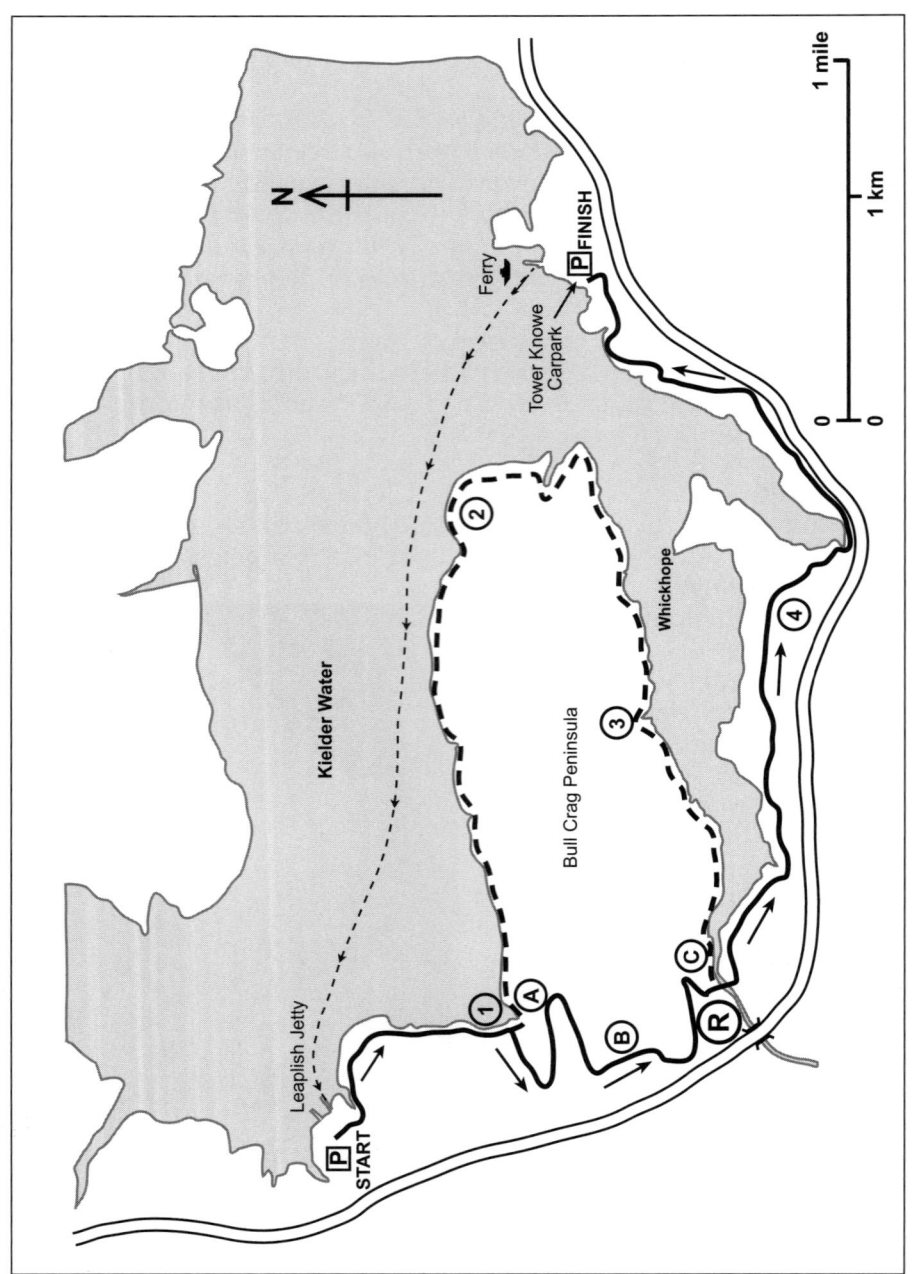

come round a bend and see – surprisingly close, across the water – Tower Knowe, where you started from.

*Don't be fooled however – there's a big inlet to walk around and you still have plenty of walking to do.*

3. After 3½ miles, or roughly one hour's walking, when you reach a fork in the path turn to your left towards the water – signposted Lakeside Way.

After ten minutes on this path, you'll reach a three-way fingerpost. Turn left, towards Tower Knowe, now just three miles away.

*There is a sign warning of a steep slope ahead – don't worry, this is aimed at the mountain bikers who use the path rather than the walkers. You may well see a few of them with white knuckles and anxious faces!*

The path now winds down delightfully through pine trees, before eventually coming to an iron bridge, which is the rendezvous point for your group.

## Low Road

1. Once you have waved goodbye to your companions you can afford 20 or 30 minutes sitting in Freya's Cabin before you have to set off. When you do start walking, return to the upper path and turn left at the signpost.

A. Follow the track uphill and it bends right so that you are now walking inland with the reservoir behind you. The wide clear track takes you through trees, starts to descend and meets a T-junction where you go right signposted Lakeside Way.

B. Follow this as it makes a left turn and becomes a sandy track with glimpses of the reservoir ahead.

C. At the signpost marked 'Lakeside Way South Shore Tower Knowe Visitor Centre 3 miles' go right, down a steep path which zig-zags through the trees. You'll see Craneclough Bridge, which is the rendezvous point.

Kielder Water

## Walking Together
Cross Craneclough Bridge and head uphill following signs to the Dam and Tower Knowe.

Follow the Lakeside Way as it passes Whickhope Boat House and Anchorage, and you gain a distant view of Kielder Dam and its valve tower.

*The dam is the main reminder that you are not looking at a natural lake but the UK's largest man-made reservoir, created after it was predicted that demand for water would out-strip supply. The controversial scheme was eventually granted planning permission in 1974. Construction took place in two stages – building the dam, and then creating the reservoir by pumping water through vast pipes 8km uphill from the River Tyne. It was opened by The Queen in 1982.*

From this viewpoint, continue walking, now back amongst the trees. The path descends to the inlet of Little Whickhope which you cross via a bridge below the C200 road.

4. Climbing up, you head left away from the road and follow the undulating track with signposts pointing to Tower Knowe. Soon you are back at the visitor centre.

# Walk 13
# Hadrian's Wall and Greenlee Lough

*This circuit takes you through the very special landscape north of Hadrian's Wall. You will experience lake shore and reed beds via a wooden walkway, cross hay meadows and open fell, and enjoy Hadrian's Wall views. Parts of the route can be extremely boggy. Both walks are similar distances, but the High Road has an arduous section along Hadrian's Wall while the Low Road follows easy footpaths and farm tracks. Also, a High Roader can go ahead and fetch the car if the Low Roaders want to avoid a final 1.4 miles. This means a High Roader needs to be the car driver.*

| Distances | High Road 7.7 miles (12.4 kms)<br>Low Road 6 miles (9.6 kms) to Steel Rigg, where you can wait for the car, or 7.5 miles (12 kms) for the full distance back to your car park |
|---|---|
| Duration | Approximately 5 hours |
| Parking | A small car park near Gibbs Hill Farm (Grid Ref NY747 690). To get there from the B6318 turn north almost opposite the National Park Visitor Centre at Once Brewed signposted 'Steel Rigg'. Go past Steel Rigg car park and after 0.6 mile turn right at a road sign 'Gibbs Hill 1 mile' and 'Gibbs Hill Farm Bed & Breakfast'. Drive over a cattle grid and onto the narrow unfenced road. Follow it downhill until you go over a little humpback bridge. Turn left onto a rough track and you'll see the fenced car park on the left. Go through the steel gate to park (nearest sat nav postcode NE47 7AP) |
| Map | Ordnance Survey Explorer Map OL 43 'Hadrian's Wall' |

## Walking Together

From the car park, turn right and head back up the lane. Turn right again over the little arched bridge and up the tarmac road until you reach the Permissive Footpath sign on your left, to Greenlee Lough Nature Reserve.

1. Go through the gate and follow the path across the field. Pass through a second gate and continue on the path. It's less distinct here, but keep near the edge of the field with the fence to your left. Continue below a gated enclosure via two kissing gates. After a while the path rises towards a five bar gate in a wall beside woods – don't go through the gate but continue towards the lake on the path with the wall on your right. It veers left and drops down towards the marsh.

2. The next section of the path is a delightful boardwalk (beware, the wooden planks are very slippery when wet). It carries you through

On the approach to Greenlee Lough

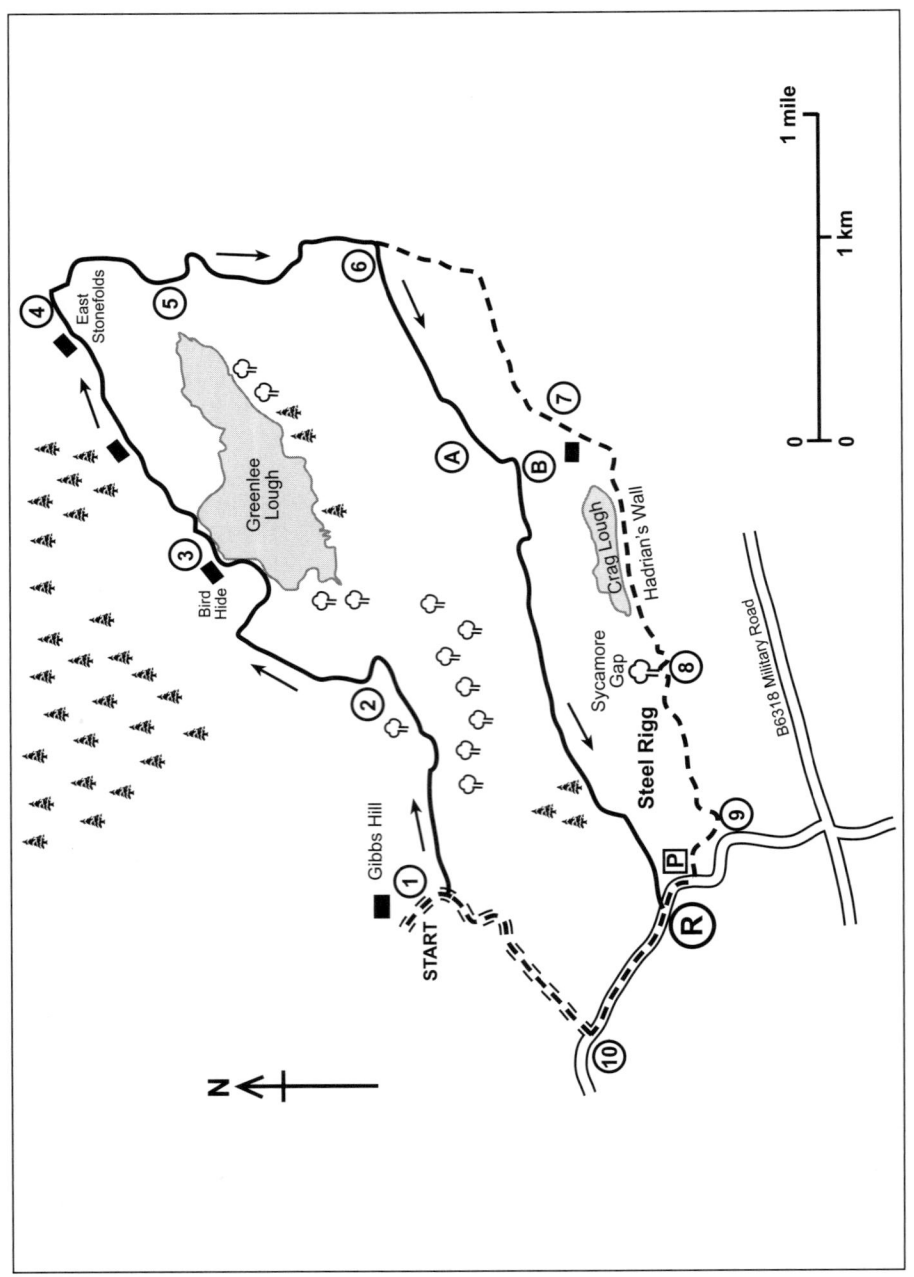

a wild wetland area, rich in wildlife, including otters and migratory birds. In summer, plants such as flag iris and marsh marigold thrive in these surroundings. When you reach a T-Junction of boardwalk paths, turn right heading towards the Lough. At the end of the boardwalk, follow the grassy path which leads round to the right with the fence on your left. Enjoy the beautiful views towards Greenlee Lough and Hadrian's Wall.

3. Go through a gate and continue on the path with a wire fence and wooded enclosure on your right. When you reach a stile on your right it's worth a detour to the bird hide on the shores of the glacial Lough. Ospreys have been seen here in recent years and it is hoped they may return to breed. Even if you don't see any rare birds, it's a lovely place to sit, catch your breath, and admire the view over the water.

    From the bird hide, re-trace your steps and go right after you've re-crossed the stile. The path soon makes a left turn, with a drystone wall on your right and reaches a three-way Public Footpath signpost. You head straight on towards Stonefolds, go over the stile quickly followed by a ladder stile and small footbridge. The path now swings to the left around a grassy mound. When you reach West Stonefolds farmhouse, go over a ladder stile set in the stone wall. The path passes in front of the house, then through a five bar gate and onto a gravel farm track which leads you to East Stonefolds farmhouse. Continue past the house and on along the track.

4. Soon you will see a gate and stone wall ahead bisecting the track, but instead of descending to it you need to turn right and go over a ladder stile with a yellow waymarker and the acorn motif which signals that you are now walking on the Pennine Way. Walk straight ahead (south) following the waymarkers, and you will pick up a distinct path heading downhill to cross a bridge and a stile. There is now a clear path for you to follow off to your right. Look for a fingerpost on the nearest hill crest. This will lead you down to a section of stone flagstones bisecting a very boggy area of ground. Keep following the Pennine Way markers.

5. Once over this section, the path begins to ascend steadily and diagonally uphill. Stay on this main track until you reach the top of the hill, where you will see a gate. Cross over a farm track and continue following the waymarkers, passing through a kissing gate beside a five bar gate. Swing round to the right on a grassy track. Keep following the Pennine Way, down and up again to a gate. Cross using the stile and on your left hand side you will see Broomlee Lough. Continue on a lovely, inviting path as the looming crags and crests topped by Hadrian's Wall become closer.

6. After a slight ascent you go right, over a ladder stile beside a five-bar gate with the remains of a lime kiln ahead. Here is where the group splits and Low Roaders head west while High Roaders go diagonally south west towards Hadrian's Wall.

## High Road

6. Head for Hadrian's Wall on the still clearly-marked Pennine Way. When you reach the Wall, cross using the ladder stile, and then turn right (west).

    *You will now follow the line of Hadrian's Wall all the way to Steel Rigg car park. This section is very up and down, but the stunning scenery makes it well worth the effort. You are now on two national trails – the Pennine Way and also the Hadrian's Wall Path which follows the World Heritage Site from Bowness-on-Solway in Cumbria to Wallsend on North Tyneside.*

7. You shortly come to Hotbank Farm.

    *The view looking towards the farm and beyond to Crag Lough is an iconic one, often seen on postcards and calendars of the area.*

    Beyond the farmhouse, you cross a farm track. Turn right here towards the Lough, over a ladder stile, and you will see a signpost pointing left into the trees, directing you towards Steel Rigg. Here you go through a lovely woodland section, which climbs up above the southern shores of Crag Lough before coming out of the trees and heading along a steep escarpment.

    *You may well see rock climbers here – but beware the steep drop!*

8. The path now plunges steeply towards the famous Sycamore Gap.

   *Or 'Kevin's Tree' as it is now known locally, ever since it featured in the film 'Robin Hood: Prince of Thieves', starring Kevin Costner.*

   Just after the sycamore tree you pass the remains of Milecastle 39.

   *Milecastles were small forts, built by the Romans roughly one mile apart along the whole of the Wall.*

   Beyond this is a steep up and down section laid with stone flags, with a final steep descent taking you towards Steel Rigg car park in the trees ahead on your right.

9. Where the path seems to go up towards a gate, don't go through the gate but stay right onto the broad grassy track heading in the direction of the car park, which is reached via a section of asphalt path. This is the busiest area on the wall, apart from Housesteads Fort.

   Rendezvous with the Low Roaders in Steel Rigg car park. Anyone who is tired could rest here and wait for the a fitter person to fetch the car! To walk back to your start point, turn right out of the carpark and follow the road downhill.

10. Turn right again at the signpost for Gibbs Hill.

    The distance from Steel Rigg back to your car is 1.4 miles.

## Low Road

6. Take the grassy path heading for the old lime kiln. Once past the kiln, keep to the right of the small plantation up ahead. Gradually the dramatic crags above Crag Lough come into view, and you veer left at the end of the plantation to reach a farm track and a waymarker.

A. Go left onto the track and walk toward Hotbank Farm.

B. Ignore the ladder stile ahead of you and cross the small stile on the right to follow a footpath across a hayfield with views of Crag Lough to your left. Cross a second stile and walk towards a fingerpost pointing you to turn right, uphill, to a ladder stile. Cross this and head uphill towards a barn. Keep to the left of the barn following the waymarkers and continue on a track with a wall to your right.

*You can now see Sycamore Gap on the left in a deep dip of Hadrian's Wall. The tree famously made an appearance in the film 'Robin Hood: Prince of Thieves' starring Kevin Costner.*

Cross the ladder stile beside a metal gate and follow the path as it veers left and becomes a stony track which leads to the tarmac road.

C. At the road go left uphill to Steel Rigg car park. This is the rendezvous point.

# Walk 14
# Hadrian's Wall: Housesteads to Cawfields and Walltown

This is a linear walk – you can either use two cars or take the Hadrian's Wall Bus Service AD122. The bus runs from Easter to October (details on the website northumberlandnationalpark.org.uk).

Hadrian's Wall can be deceptively tiring to walk because of steep ascents and descents and uneven stones underfoot alongside the Wall. An easier grassy path runs parallel on the south side. This is the Military Way, a former supply road used by the Romans. Low Roaders can use this to bypass some of the harder sections while rejoining the High Roaders beside Hadrian's Wall for the most spectacular views and Roman remains. This means that unlike the other walks in the book, there are several points where the group splits up then gets back together again. The Low Roaders catch the Hadrian's Wall Bus back to the car, leaving the High Roaders to walk the final three miles.

| Distances | High Road 8.9 miles (14.3 kms)<br>Low Road 6.2 miles (10 kms) |
|---|---|
| Duration | Approximately 6¼ hours |
| Parking | If using two cars – leave one at Walltown Car Park (grid reference NY 670660, nearest sat nav postcode CA8 7JB) and all travel in the other to Housesteads Roman Fort (grid reference NY 794684). Both car parks are pay and display, both have toilets and refreshments. Or, if you are absolutely confident the Hadrian's Wall Bus timetable suits your timings, you can use just one car and leave it at Walltown then all catch the bus to Housesteads |
| Map | Ordnance Survey Explorer Map OL 43 'Hadrian's Wall' |

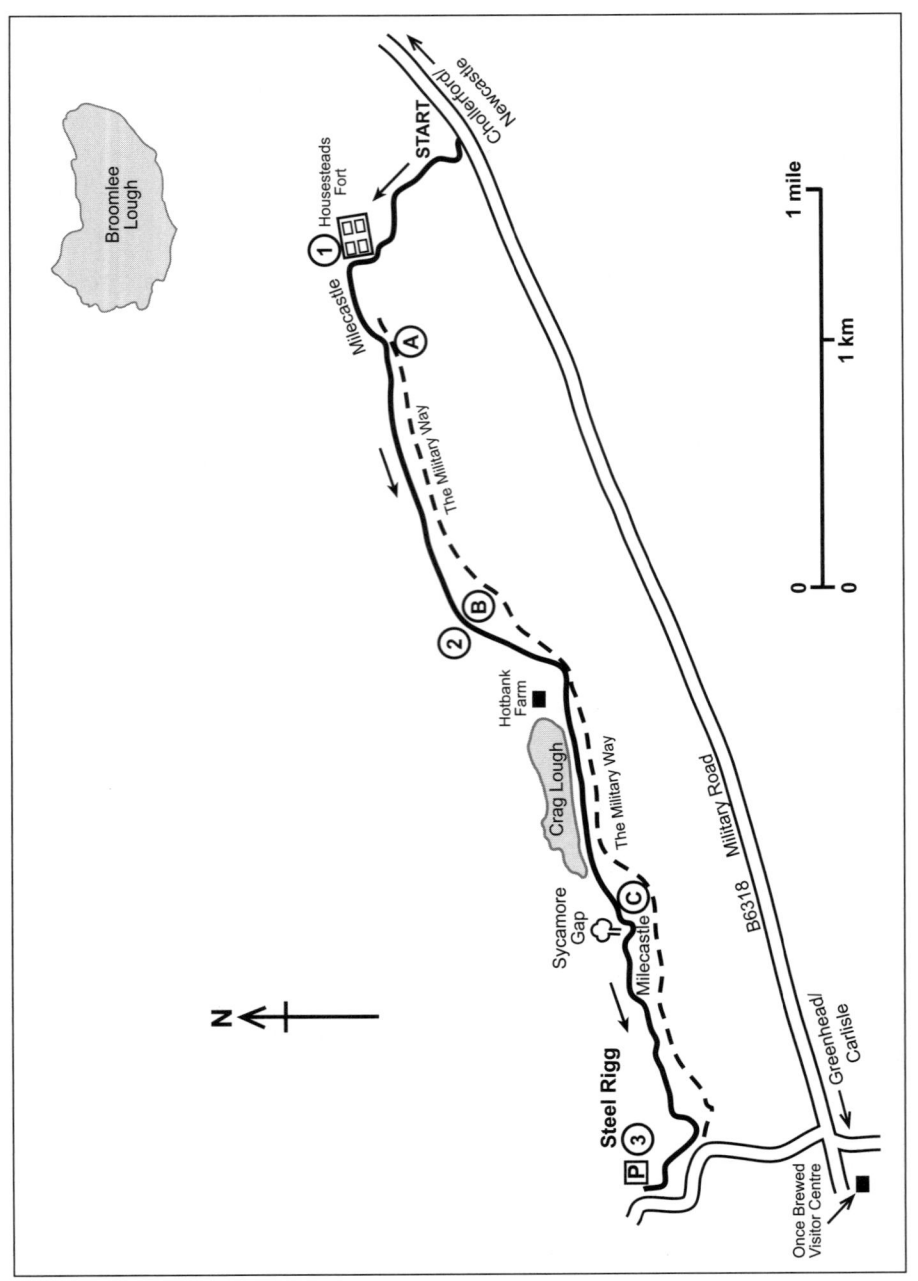

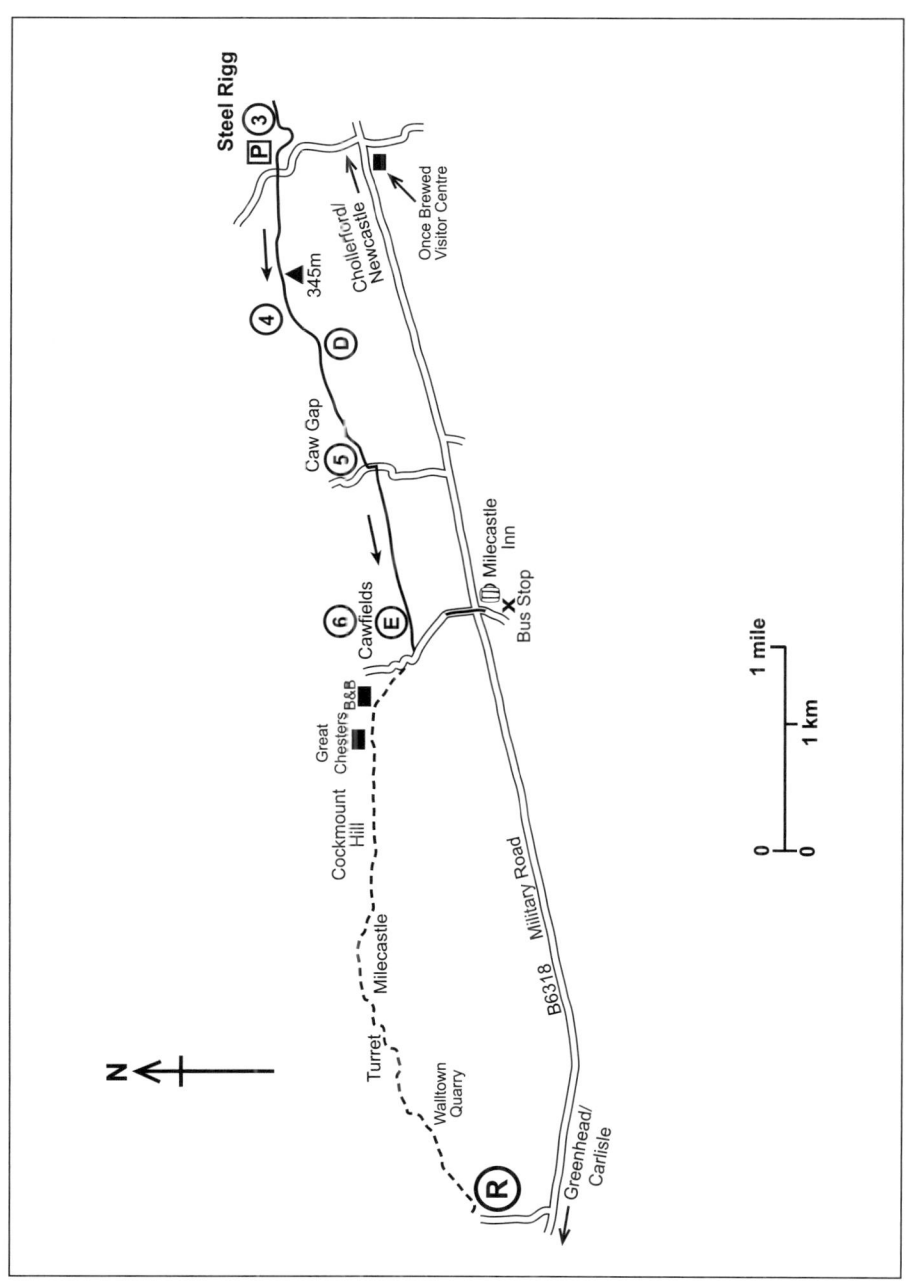

## Walking Together
From the visitor centre go through a kissing gate and along the track.

*You only need to pay the entrance fee if you are going into the fort.*

The track dips down then up towards the fort. Continue straight up the hill on the grass, to the left of the fort wall. Go through the small gate ahead and you are now on Hadrian's Wall.

1. Turn left through the trees and either stay on the main path or, if you have a good head for heights, choose the narrow path parallel to it on the right. There is a steep drop on one side. To the north are views of Broomlee Lough.

   Go through a small gate and walk along the grassy path beside the Roman Wall to reach a milecastle.

   *One of these fortlets was built at every Roman mile along the Wall and they accommodated up to 30 soldiers.*

## First Split Point
A. After the milecastle the High Roaders stay beside Hadrian's Wall and the Low Roaders veer left to follow the inviting grassy path of the Military Way until it reaches a clump of trees on the left with a glimpse of the waters of Crag Lough ahead. Here the Low Roaders head back up to the Wall to **rendezvous at B** with the High Roaders for the descent past Hotbank Farm.

## Walking Together
After a short section of flagstones, go through a gate and across the farm driveway.

2. Go right over the ladder stile and immediately left up through a small wood. Back out in the open you are rewarded with views down to Crag Lough and to Wark Forest in the north.

   *Then a steep descent takes you down to Sycamore Gap and the famous tree that featured in an early scene of the film 'Robin Hood: Prince of Thieves'. Kevin Costner and Morgan Freeman rescued a young boy from the Sheriff's men after he had climbed up into the tree.*

Sycamore Gap on Hadrian's Wall

## Second Split Point

C. At the sycamore tree is another opportunity for Low Roaders to leave the Wall itself and pick up the Military Way by walking down past the baby sycamore in its protective stone circle and turning right. High Roaders head up the steep hill beside Hadrian's Wall and continue to follow it to reach Steel Rigg car park for the next **rendezvous point** (3).

Low Roaders will once again be on the grassy track of the Military Way, which descends along a short stony section then swings right, uphill and reverts to a grassy surface. Go through a gate to the right of Peel Cottage.

If any of the party wants to bail out at this point and catch the bus from Once Brewed it's only a short walk from here down the tarmac road to the National Park Visitor Centre. Otherwise, turn right uphill from the cottage and a few yards further on you go through a little gate between two big stone gateposts.

3. Turn left and walk up the wide grassy track to **rendezvous** at Steel Rigg car park (3).

## Walking Together

Leave the car park and go left along the tarmac road for a few yards, then turn right and through a kissing gate to walk up a gradually ascending grassy field alongside Hadrian's Wall.

4. A trig point marks the highest point of the Wall's entire length, on Windshields Crags 1,130 feet. From the trig point continue alongside Hadrian's Wall. You will encounter several steep descents and ascents, but there is again an alternative to the south.

## Third Split Point

D. This comes when the group reaches a small gate with the sign 'end of access land' near a step stile on the right with a hand grip cemented on top of the wall. To take the detour Low Roaders go through the gate, then turn left using an indistinct path alongside a stone wall down and up a dip. As you crest the dip, veer right and the track becomes much more obvious. Follow it down until it turns right before the linear earthworks of the Vallum.

*The Vallum is a unique feature on any Roman frontier. It is a huge ditch with earth mounds which runs the entire length of the Roman Wall.*

The path can be boggy in places, but is mainly a pleasant grassy track leading towards stone outcrops and the Bogle Hole. This is an interesting and atmospheric spot.

*A bogle is a ghost or goblin or creature from folklore. History doesn't relate whether a bogle lives here, but there are the remains of a dozen shielings dating from the 15th and 16th centuries. These were huts which were used as temporary homes by people who brought their livestock up from the Tyne Valley to graze in the summer.*

The grassy path leads to a ladder stile onto the road at Caw Gap. Cross the road and over another stile to follow a signpost 'Cawfields 1'. This is another wide grassy track parallel to the Roman Wall, and as you look up at the Wall against the skyline you get an idea of what an imposing feature it was.

E. As you near the sharp triangular rock face of Cawfields Quarry turn left to follow another field path south, and eventually out onto the lane. Turn left towards the Milecastle Inn, cross the B6318, and the bus stop you need is beside the pub garden.

5. High Roaders stay beside the Roman Wall, crossing over the lane at Caw Gap and passing Caw Gap turret which was a watchtower on the Wall.

   As you crest a hill you can see Cawfields quarry, lake and car park ahead of you. If the group hasn't split up before, this is where Low Roaders will leave to catch the bus back to Walltown. Before going through the gate at the milecastle the Low Roaders go south along a grassy path to reach the bus stop at the Milecastle Inn. If they miss the bus they could wait at the pub for the High Roaders to come along in the car later.

6. High Roaders go through the gate and along the path beside the water-filled quarry and into the car park where there are toilets. Exit the car park and turn left onto the tarmac lane for a short while, cross a stone bridge and pick up the path with a signpost 'Walltown Quarry 3¼ miles'.

   Go over a stone stile and up the grassy path in front of a farmhouse B&B and continue on through the field ahead. Cross the ladder stile and continue on over the next field to another ladder stile, then across another field to the next ladder stile. You have now reached Great Chesters Farm. Follow the path as it curves to the right past the farm buildings.

   *Look out here for the remains of Aesica Roman Fort, although these are somewhat diminished by their proximity to the farm buildings.*

Stay on the grassy path towards another ladder stile, and after the next ladder stile go straight on towards the derelict buildings of Cockmount Hill in a clump of trees, then on to another ladder stile beside a five-bar gate.

The path now winds delightfully through woodland until you cross a ladder stile onto open moorland. Follow the steadily-rising grass path with the wall to your right.

At a junction of drystone walls cross the ladder stile and continue on straight ahead. The route now drops steeply to a stone step stile in a drystone wall and rises steeply on the other side.

7. After a long steep section down stone steps you reach a pretty area of marshland and wildflowers where stone flags have been laid across the boggy bits. Cross another stile and head uphill.

   *The next section of the Wall is dramatic but delicate. Walkers are asked to keep to the left of the crags, not only because of the drop but also in order to protect the fragile rubble rigg – that's the stone left over from the Wall. This was re-constructed in places during the Victorian era.*

   Once you have enjoyed the lofty views, cut inland and keep slightly to the left of the line of the wall, following the line of the crags up above.

8. Beyond Walltown Crag Turret 45A you will reach a T-junction of walls – turn left here and walk slightly downhill with the wall on your right and beyond that Walltown Quarry and lake.

   You reach a broad gravel track which will take you back to the visitor centre. After a kissing gate turn sharp right onto a broad path, when you reach a fork in the path with the lake on your left, take the left hand fork to reach the car park where the Low Roaders should be waiting.

# Walk 15
# Blanchland and The Carriers' Way

*These routes treat you to one of Northumberland's most attractive villages, which is frequently used as a film location, and some fine moorland scenery. Mostly on good paths through woodland and heather, with a riverbank finale, both walks provide wide views after a steady climb. Neither route is suitable for dogs – the paths cross a grouse shooting estate and dogs are banned.*

| Distances | High Road 9.5 miles (15.3 km)<br>Low Road 6.5 miles (10.5 km) |
|---|---|
| Duration | Approximately 5 hours |
| Parking | Car park in Blanchland (nearest sat nav postcode DH8 9ST), pay at honesty box where a donation of £1 is suggested. Grid reference NY964504 |
| Maps | Ordnance Survey Explorer Map OL 43 'Hadrian's Wall' and Explorer Map 307 'Consett & Derwent Reservoir' |

## Walking Together

You could just turn left out of the car park and head up the tarmac road, however, a far nicer parallel route is to cross the lane to a fingerpost pointing left along a path into the woods. This is a more attractive and interesting route. Follow the narrow path, turning left slightly uphill through woodland.

Where the path forks, at a marker post, keep left, basically heading straight ahead of you, uphill through the trees. At a broken down gateway keep straight on following a yellow footpath arrow. After approximately ten minutes walking up a relatively steep hill you reach a forestry track with a fingerpost. Turn left following the yellow waymarker.

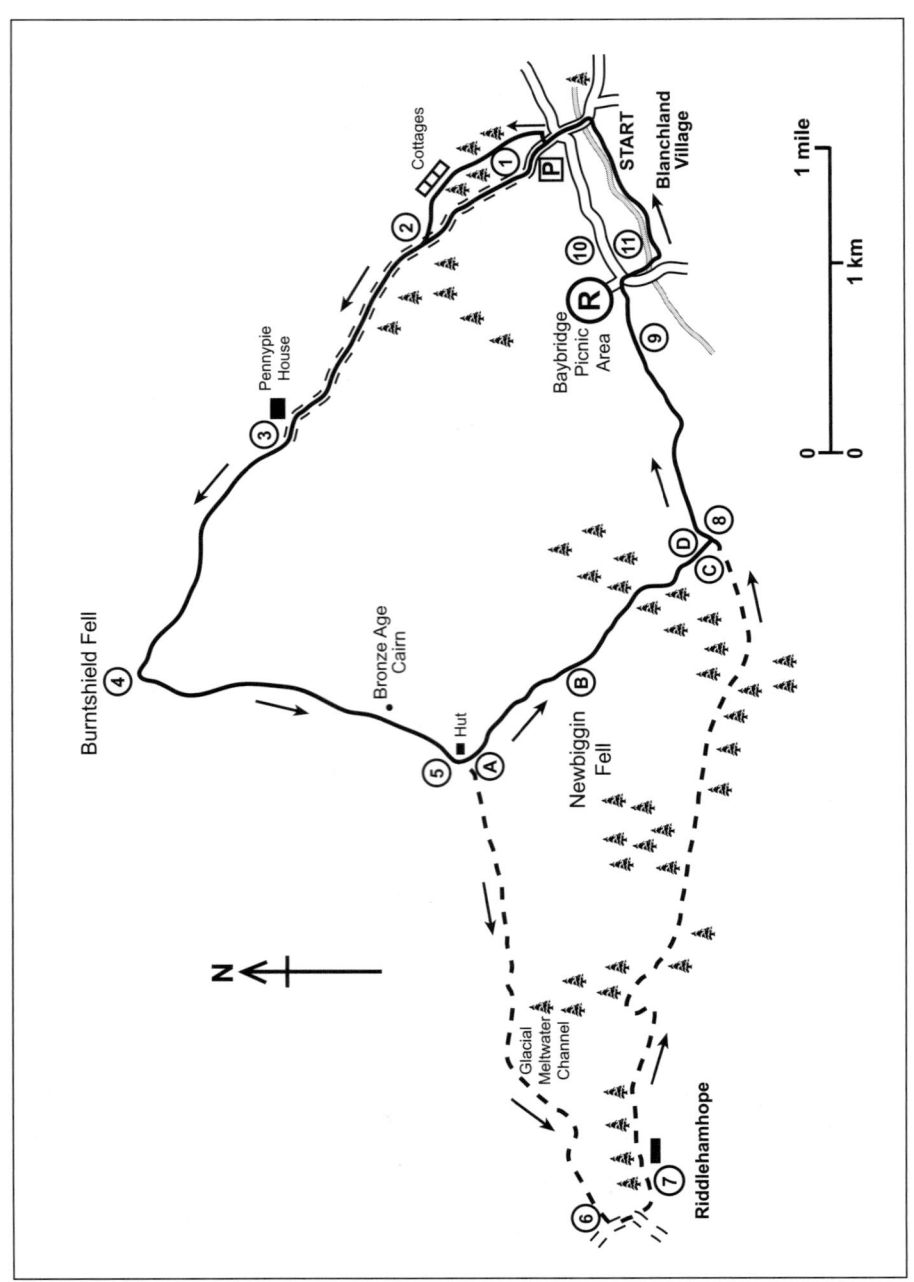

1. After a short time you reach a 'No Access' sign. The alternative footpath route is clearly marked, turning to the right and then immediately left through a gate. The path skirts along the edge of a wire fence and then drops down to a gate. Go past a woodshed and in front of a row of houses, the surviving cottages of the former lead-mining village of Shildon.

2. The track brings you onto a tarmac lane (this is the road that you could have walked directly up from the car park if you had chosen that option).

   *You will see the remains of Shildon Engine House which housed a steam-driven engine to pump water from lead mines deep underground. Mining declined after the mid 19th century and the engine house fell into disrepair, but its remains have been preserved to help tell the story of an industry that used to dominate the North Pennines landscape.*

   Ignore a fingerpost pointing to Blanchland Moor, continuing instead uphill along the road.

   *Listen out for lapwings and curlews on this stretch, they inhabit these moors, coming inland to breed in the summertime. Disused mine shafts, sink holes and old mine workings dot this landscape – another remnant of the area's mining past. They are mostly fenced off, as the small tree-filled enclosure on the left of the track.*

3. Towards the end of the track, Pennypie House comes into view ahead of you on the right.

   *This is a classic low-built Northumberland farmhouse, which reputedly sold pies for a penny to passing lead miners and drovers.*

   Walk straight on through the gate to the left of Pennypie House where a fingerpost signals the start of the moorland section of this walk. Head uphill to the right on a wide track and almost immediately you'll see a sign pointing to Burntshield Haugh. Turn off the track here and walk though the heather of Bulbeck Common.

The path takes you across the moor with marker posts guiding you along the way – if in doubt, look for a ladder stile over the drystone wall ahead of you.

*The ground here is dotted with grouse shooting butts, some wooden, and some more solid stone structures. The shooting season runs from "the glorious" 12th of August until the 10th December, and all year round these moors are managed specifically for grouse. The birds feed on young heather but need older taller plants when breeding. You will see distinct patches on the moorland where heather has been burned to encourage new growth or left long for nesting.*

When you reach the wall, use the ladder stile and then walk straight on across the broad track and carry on in the same direction, following the way-markers which continue through the heather ahead of you. This part of the walk can be wet in places, so choose your route carefully.

As the track starts to go slightly downhill you will see a shed just ahead of you, with a red corrugated iron roof. Continue on, not towards the shed but straight ahead, aiming for a broad track which crosses your footpath. Here there is a waymarker with several blue arrows – you are now on a bridleway called the Carriers' Way.

4. On reaching this track, turn left.

   *In the 18th century this track would have been busy with pack ponies doing the heavy haulage of the lead mining and smelting industries. The roads were too bad for carts so lead was carried from the remote upland mines by lines of up to twenty small sturdy ponies controlled by one mounted man.*

   The broad grassy track contours around the hill, with fabulous open views, and brings you to a stone wall and gate. Go through the gate and continue straight ahead. After a while you pass a way-marker and path going left – ignore this and continue straight ahead towards a stone hut which should now be visible on the horizon ahead.

Follow the path past a gas-pipeline marked by a cairn.

*This may seem odd but has a serious purpose – the post warns anyone who might be considering excavating here that there is a gas pipeline, and asking them to telephone before digging. Just beyond this is the rather more exciting site of a large Bronze-Age cairn. When this was excavated in 1997, remains of human bodies were discovered.*

5. When you reach the hut you might decide this is a good lunch spot – it is mainly used by shooting parties but if it is free it offers shelter and benches to sit on. To the north you can see Hexham race course and the Cheviot Hills beyond. The hut is your split point for this walk

Blanchland Moor

## High Road

Walk uphill from the hut and go right for a very short distance along a wide track. Almost immediately turn left onto a grassy track. You are now back on the Carriers' Way.

The path is indistinct in places but just continue in the same direction and on the same contour until you come close to a conifer plantation. Before you reach the trees, bear right and pick up a narrow path which takes you around the deep gully to your left.

*This unexpected and rather dramatic feature is in fact a glacial meltwater channel. Bizarrely, water here would have flowed uphill, due to the pressure of being underneath the ice.*

The path skirts around this steep-sided gully before leading you onto a section of wooden boards across a boggy section of ground. Continue over the stile and up the other side of the hill. The path rises up steeply through bracken. At the top of the hill pick up a yellow waymarker directing you on through the heather towards a clump of trees on the horizon.

Head to the right of the trees and before too long you will reach a fence with a stile.

6. Cross the fence and then turn left onto the broad gravel track.

   Where the track bears to the right (signed Heathery Burn) do not follow it. Instead keep straight ahead and go through a five-bar gate. Follow the broad grassy track down to your left towards another gate.

7. Go through this and pass in front of the ruined building of Riddlehamhope.

   *This was a Victorian hunting lodge, and at its western end are the remains of a bastle (a fortified farmhouse) which probably dates back to the 16th or 17th Century.*

   Pass through another couple of gates and continue straight ahead, with woodland on your left. At the end of the woods, cross the wall

Riddlehamhope

using the ladder stile. The path now heads gently downhill. It becomes steeper before entering a conifer plantation via a ladder stile.

Exit the woodland through a gate and continue straight ahead along a gravel track gradually downhill towards another wooded area for around 10-15 minutes. Stay on the track through the woodland and go through a metal gate.

8. Continue on and ignore a gate on your right with a footpath sign. Instead go through another metal gate. You will now be walking with a stone wall and trees on your right. Go through another (red) metal gate. The path heads slightly downhill, and round in front of a large house. Go through a wooden gate and then continue straight on down a tarmac lane.

*117*

9. When you arrive at the tiny hamlet of Baybridge, turn right to reach the Picnic Area just before the road bridge. Here you are meeting your friends.

## Low Road

5. You can afford to linger at the hut for a good 20-30 minutes after your High Road companions have set off. When you finally tear yourself away from such a lovely spot, walk uphill from the hut and you meet a broad track.

A. Go left through the large wooden gate and head along a wide sandy track with views down into the valley.

B. The track leads to a conifer plantation where you go through a gate and downhill through the trees until a left hand bend delivers you to a steel gate and into a field.

C. Turn right in the field and walk down towards the right hand corner and a wooden gate with a yellow marker pointing you downhill. Through the wooden gate, you walk down the field with the stone wall on your left.

D. At the farm track you go left through the red metal gate. Your High Road colleagues will also return along this track, but a more obvious and comfortable rendezvous point lies further on, so continue along to pass the farm and house at Newbiggin. The track takes you to a wooden gate with a tarmac lane beyond, which continues downhill.

E. At the road junction at the end of the lane you turn right, go past the Jubilee bench and just after the County Durham road sign turn right into Baybridge picnic site, which is the rendezvous location.

## Walking Together

You now have a choice of two routes back to Blanchland each offering different delights – both follow the river, but one is close to the water the other is higher up and through woodland.

For the riverbank route north of the river, leave the picnic site and cross the road to join a boardwalk at the signpost 'Blanchland ¾ mile

Carrick 2½ miles'. Through the gap in the stone wall the path turns right and you have a lovely walk along the river bank, weaving between trees. After you pass a playground you reach a grassy area, cross a wooden bridge and you're in the village. There are public toilets on the other side of the road. Walk up away from the river and through the village square – a picturesque scene that has been used as the location for several period films. Blanchland has a shop, a pub, a tea room, a hat shop and an Abbey. You'll recognise the lane up to the left of the tea room which leads to the car park.

Or, for the woodland route, when you leave Baybridge picnic site turn right onto the road and go over the bridge. Turn left at the green metal Public Footpath sign and head into the woods. Follow the 'Pennine Journey' waymarkers straight on, along a wide smooth track. The route undulates through the woods, passing a waterfall cascading down dramatic crags on your right. Eventually you follow yellow waymarkers taking you behind a cottage and out to the road. Turn left and walk into the village.

# Walk 16
# South Tyne Trail and Pennine Way

*Low Road walkers love former railway lines with their gentle gradients and smooth surfaces, and the South Tyne Trail is an exceptionally enjoyable railway line. To please the High Roaders there's also a section of Pennine Way, and both routes include a magnificent viaduct over the River South Tyne.*

| Distances | High Road 6.3 miles (10.1km)<br>Low Road 4.9 miles (7.9 kms) |
|---|---|
| Duration | Approximately 3 hours |
| Parking | This is a two-car walk to give you a good length of the old railway line or the Pennine Way. Leave one vehicle at the South Tyne Trail car park for Lambley Viaduct a little north west of Coanwood, grid reference NY 679595 (nearest sat nav postcode NE49 0NX). The group then continues in the second vehicle to Slaggyford, further south on the A689. Turn right in the village at the brown sign for 'Yew Tree Chapel' and go up the little lane until you see the station platform. Park near the South Tyne Trail footpath sign, grid reference NY 676524 |
| Map | Ordnance Survey Explorer Map OL 43 'Hadrian's Wall' |

## Walking Together
Set off northwards along the South Tyne Trail with the station platform on your left and the former stationmaster's house on your right. A short way along don't be confused where the track appears to fork – you keep to the left and continue straight on.

It is easy, level walking with classic North Pennines views on either side, and a few relic railway features.

On the South Tyne Trail

*The Haltwhistle to Alston line opened in the 1850s, primarily to carry lead from the mines in the Alston area but it was also a passenger line until 1976. Engineers faced many challenges building the 13-mile route – it climbs from 400 feet to 1,000 feet above sea level and crosses the River South Tyne three times. There are also viaducts over seven tributaries. You will marvel at the biggest viaduct later in the walk.*

1. At around two miles from Slaggyford the character of the walk changes as the trail passes into woodland.

2. Where you emerge from Softley Low Wood and into open pasture you'll see a four-way fingerpost, a bench and an information panel near Whitwham Farm. This is where the party splits.

## High Road

2. At the bench turn left, following the sign which says Whitwham Walk. This route takes you down across a stile and over a field. There is no clear path but head uphill and diagonally to the left following the tree line. Eventually you will see a ladder stile which crosses the wall onto the main road the A689. Take care when crossing – this road can have fast traffic.

   Cross the ladder stile on the far side of the road. Walk straight ahead to the top of the field. You will pick up a waymarker post with yellow arrows and the acorn motif which indicates that you are now on the Pennine Way.

3. Turn right and walk on the Pennine Way for around 1.5 miles with a drystone wall and then a fence on your left. You will cross four stiles.

   *From up here, there are lovely sweeping views – with the South Tyne valley ahead and the brooding hills of the North Pennines behind you. Underfoot is typical Pennine Way, ie wet in places. There are some boards across the worst sections but you may still need to make minor detours of your own.*

   After around 20-30 minutes walking, you should be able to see a road and village ahead. Ignoring paths off to the left, continue straight on and down the hill, crossing a ladder stile which takes you onto the road.

On the Pennine Way

4. Cross the road and turn immediately right onto a small road signposted Featherstone. Walk in front of a terrace of houses. The last house actually has a footpath running through its garden! Go onto the driveway of the house – it is signposted Lambley – and walk down the path with the garage on your right, over a stile and into a field.

*These open, tranquil pastures were once massively industrialised. Scores of men worked in mining and coke manufacture and in 1799 the Earl of Carlisle opened a waggonway to carry the goods east to Brampton, hauled by horses. Soon the line was re-laid with iron rails and gradually upgraded to carry steam trains. In 1837 Stephenson's famous Rocket was used to haul coal on Lord Carlisle's Railway.*

Continue straight on over the next three fields (crossing the fences via a stile, a kissing gate and a five-bar gate). Then go through a

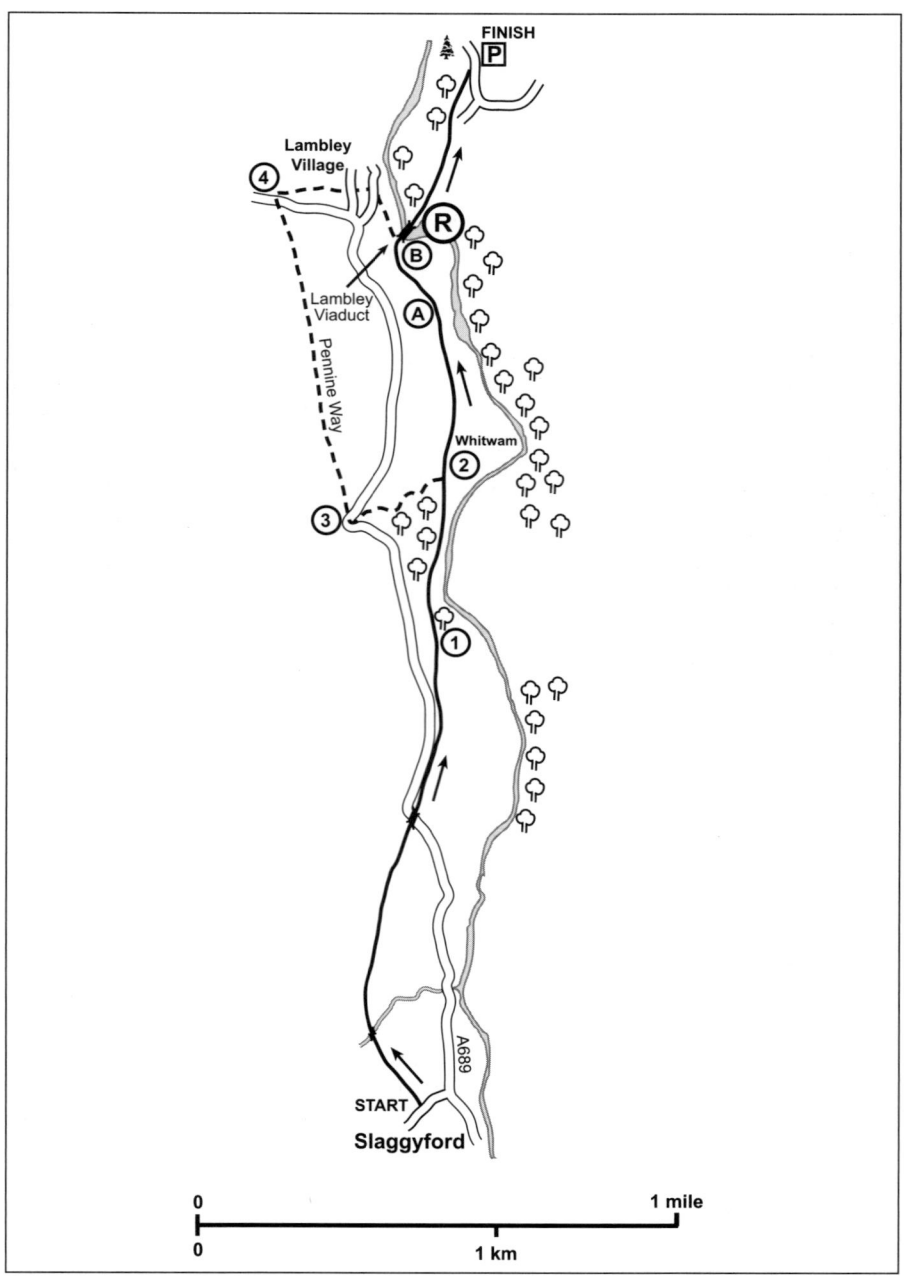

tunnel which takes you underneath the Coanwood road. A short way after the underpass the path forks – go right and continue onto the road. Head straight across here, looking for a footpath sign to Lambley Viaduct. Tyne View cottage should be on your left.

This path then turns right behind a row of cottages before entering a delightful wooded section and descending via steps to the viaduct. When you come to a four-way fingerpost make sure you don't continue going downhill! You want to take the path signed South Tyne Trail via Lambley Viaduct.

To do so, turn right and head uphill and onto the viaduct itself, where you will rendezvous with the low-roaders.

## Low Road

2. You will have plenty of time for an extra rest on the bench after your companions set off. When you are ready to leave, continue northwards through a gate and along the track with Whitwham Farm buildings down to your right. Simply follow the track, your way enlivened by the sounds of streams and waterfalls passing under the rail line and birdsong from the farmland and trees on either side. Soon you reach a bench which offers a narrow view between the trees of the east bank of the river with its dense mixed woodland cover. Worthy of another little rest.

A. Eventually the track reaches a tarmac lane and a red brick house, and to the right of the house is your first glimpse of Lambley Viaduct. The South Tyne trail is signposted straight over the lane and you continue along for a short distance until you get to a fingerpost with signs for South Tyne Trail North, Lambley Viaduct, Lambley Village and Haltwhistle.

B. Here the rail line passes through private property so the footpath diverts down to the right via steps to skirt the garden boundary.

*Be aware that on the OS Explorer OL 43 Hadrian's Wall map the right of way along the trail depicted by green lozenge symbols is incorrectly shown as continuing past the private house. The advantage of the detour down towards the river is that you pass under one of the viaduct arches, giving a dramatic angle on the amazing structure.*

*125*

After passing under the viaduct you turn left up a steep stepped slope to reach a four-way fingerpost. Your High Road companions will be coming down from the direction of Lambley village, but a nicer rendezvous point is further on, so you turn left along the level path with handrails to reach the metal staircase which takes you up onto the viaduct.

Because the valley is steep-sided, as you ascend the steps you quickly feel as though you are in the tree canopy, then once you're on the viaduct there is much to see in all directions.

*Lambley Viaduct is a stunning feat of Victorian engineering. It has thirteen spans rising to 100 feet and was built in 1852 to carry trains laden with lead, coal and limestone. After the rail line closed in 1976 the condition of the viaduct deteriorated until it was restored by the British Rail Property Board. It is now owned by the North Pennines Heritage Trust.*

You'll want to linger along the length of the viaduct, before heading to the northern end where you'll see a bench and an information panel. This is the rendezvous point.

## Walking Together
From the bench continue northwards along the track. You pass a signpost pointing to Lambley Footbridge which is the little bridge you saw down at river level below you from the viaduct. This is the site of Coanwood Station, with the remains of a platform.

Carry on along the South Tyne Trail until it crosses a road and you have reached the car park where you left your other vehicle.

# Also from Sigma Leisure:

### Discover Northumberland
### 30 coastal and inland walks
*Mark Lejk*

30 circular walks covering the whole of Northumberland from north to south and east to west aimed at people of all walking abilities and preferences with lengths ranging from 4.5 km (2.8 miles) to 17.8 km (11.1 miles) and difficulty ranging from easy to strenuous. Many of the longer walks have shorter versions and altogether the different variations and combinations make for 48 routes. The walks range from the fabulous Northumberland coastline to the Cheviot Hills, Kielder Forest, the North Pennines, Hadrian's Wall and there are a significant number of walks in the area between the coast and the Cheviots.

*£8.99*

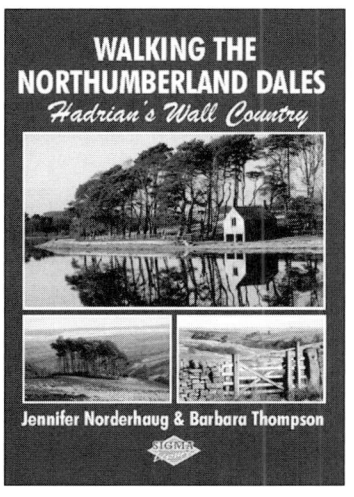

### Walking the Northumberland Dales
### Hadrian's Wall Country
*Norderhaug & Thompson*

This guidebook explores the lesser-known landscapes of North and South Tynedale, Allendale, Hexhamshire, Blanchland and Hadrian's Wall, all within easy access of Newcastle-upon-Tyne, Durham and other popular locations. The walks are packed with interest on the history, industrial archaeology, traditions, and culture of the area.

*£7.95*

## Discovering NewcastleGateshead
A walking guide to NewcastleGateshead plus parkland strolls and visits to coastal attractions
*Peter Donaghy & John Laidler*

26 carefully crafted walks lead to places of historical, architectural and social interest, at times through nooks and crannies that may be new even to long-standing residents. The walks are of varying lengths with opportunities for internal visits and refreshments. To involve children in the discovery process, a number of quiz questions have been included.
**£10.99**

## Walking the Cheviots
Classic Circular Routes
*Edward Baker*

This book provides an excellent introduction to this solitary, wild countryside. Everyone is catered for from weekend family walkers to the experienced hill walker with all the walks personally checked and trod by the author. Each route contains details of the natural history, geology and archaeology of the area. For ease of reference, the book is in two sections, covering the northern and southern Cheviots - distinct areas with their own unique character. There are almost 50 walks - by far the most comprehensive collection published for the Cheviots.
**£9.99**

All of our books are available through booksellers. For a free catalogue, please contact:
**Sigma Leisure, Stobart House, Pontyclerc
Penybanc Road, Ammanford SA18 3HP
Tel: 01269 593100  Fax: 01269 596116**

info@sigmapress.co.uk          www.sigmapress.co.uk